THE TARGET

A STORY OF LOVE, FAITH AND DEATH IN THE OIL FIELD

D1316503

Marilyn M. Wheeler

The Target: A Story of Love, Faith and a Supernatural Life in the Oil Field
Copyright © 2017 Marilyn Wheeler

ISBN: 978-168031-129-7

Published by Harrison House Publishers
Tulsa, OK 74145
www.harrisonhouse.com

Cover design: Joe Redmond

ENDORSEMENTS

The Al Wheeler family has been my friends for years and years. Al gave me a one of a kind horse head ring that I still treasure today. Al didn't like wasting money talking long distance on the phone, but shortly before he left us, we talked maybe a couple of hours. We talked about God, about the Holy Land he wanted to visit, about God's plan for our lives and many things I don't remember. I do remember, he talked freely and didn't care about the time, which was unusual.

Al's wife, Marilyn, has written this book about how God's plan worked in their lives. I know some unusual things happened. But I have always found the Wheelers to be truthful and upright. Al, whom I called 007, told me about some events that were like James Bond stuff.

As you read this book, you will fall in love with Marilyn Wheeler, as we did so many years ago. Remember, before you were born, God had your master plan in place.

The manuscript came to me about 10:00 p.m. and I thought I would read a couple of chapters before going to bed. I couldn't stop and finished it up about midnight.

I cried when the Wheelers cried and laughed when they laughed and was amazed at the things that happened to them.

My friends the Wheelers have been through a lot and this book will help you have a victorious life when the devil tries to TARGET you. I'm getting extra copies for my friends as it may be the book that will help you target the devil and come through situations in victory.

Ken Gaub, Ken Gaub Ministries,
Yakima, Washington

For years, as editor of Publications for Kenneth E Hagin, I heard him prophesy about the coming great move of God. One often mentioned, supernatural happening that would be an integral part of the move was "translations." Like Philip in the book of Acts, people would be transported from one place to another.

Al Wheeler experienced a most remarkable translation from Kansas in mid-America to the jungles of Uganda and back. A young African boy's life was forever changed from darkness to light as a result. Al's wife, Marilyn, has put the account into this book, something I have been hoping for years that she would do.

Dr. Billye Brim, Founder,
Billye Brim Ministries

ACKNOWLEDGMENTS

I wish to acknowledge my beloved son Steven Wheeler and daughter Brynda Wheeler for their invaluable assistance in remembering the lifetime of memories outlined in this book.

I would also like to thank Kenneth Copeland, Billye Brim and Ken Gaub for their personal encouragement and prayers in pursuing my dream of documenting Al's and my life's journey.

Additionally, a huge thank you to my granddaughter, Breahna Wheeler, and my "Girl Friday," Denise Claudio, in orchestrating the book cover and keeping me on schedule!

If not for all the wonderful people mentioned above, and too many to mention personally, *The Target* would not have come to fruition.

I am forever grateful and blessed.

With my love,

Marilyn M. Wheeler

DEDICATION

This book is lovingly dedicated to my youngest daughter, Sandi Wheeler Turner, who unexpectedly went to be with the Lord Jesus on Christmas Day 2015. The loss of her vibrant life, caring heart and genuine love has left a hole in my heart that can never be filled.

CONTENTS

FOREWORD

"Marilyn Wheeler's new book, *The Target,* is not only the story of a wonderful American Christian family that everyone will enjoy immensely, it goes to the heart of one of the most asked questions on earth, especially among Christians: Why, how, and where was God when this happened to me?

"Marilyn is a longtime personal friend of Gloria's and mine. Reading *The Target* brought her even closer to us. You need to know this strong woman of faith the way we do."

—Kenneth Copeland, Founder, Kenneth Copeland Ministries

CHAPTER 1

HOW DARE YOU DO THIS TO ME?

Albert Wheeler was an Oklahoma oil man, and I loved him. His commitment to the oil field began at the early age of fifteen and never stopped growing. Each one of us are gifted to succeed at different tasks, and he had a knack for oil and gas. He was made to hunt for oil! Yet, it's one thing to discover oil, and another thing to get the oil out of the ground. Al had the unique ability to do that. In many ways, his success in the oil field determined the direction of our lives. It opened doors of opportunity and resulted in tremendous blessings.

From the moment we began dating and seriously began to consider marriage, it was obvious from the way Albert talked of his dreams for the future that the search for oil and gas would be a dominating factor in our lives. And it was! As soon as he finished his service in the military, we began chasing his dream of success in the oil field.

Our Lives Revolved Around the Oil Field

Al quickly worked his way up the chain as he gained knowledge and experience in the oil and gas industry, until he became one of the most respected production recovery men in the oil business. His dream took us from our home in southwest Oklahoma to Farmington, New Mexico; back to Oklahoma City; then to Hill City, Kansas; to Enid, Oklahoma; to Tulsa, Oklahoma; and finally to the small Oklahoma town of Kingfisher.

We purchased a beautiful historic house on Main Street and made Kingfisher our new home. Kingfisher was perfect for us because of its size and location. It was near many of the most active oil fields in Oklahoma. The house needed a lot of work but by the time we finished remodeling and filling it with a mixture of antiques and new furnishings, the house was wonderful. I thought I would always live in that special house.

During this time, we were established in the oil business and experienced great success. Al lavishly provided for our family and was at the place in his career that he could take the jobs he wanted—without moving our family time and time again. Our three children were young at the time, and we wanted them to grow up in a small town away from the busy pace of a big city.

Much of our lives revolved around Al's schedule. During most weeks, he left early Monday morning to drive to the current well he was completing, and if he could, he would return home every night. However, if the well was too far away, he would not return until late Friday night. This became his routine so I busied myself with my children, a group of great friends, and of course our beloved Nazarene church. Since we all lived in Kingfisher, we were together almost every day.

As our son, Steve, grew up, he studied petroleum geology at the University of Oklahoma. He became successful in his own right and purchased a gorgeous home in Kingfisher also. Brynda, one of our daughters, received her degree in counseling from the University of Central Oklahoma, and opened an upscale women's shop. She also purchased her own beautiful home in Kingfisher. Our youngest daughter, Sandi, got married and was living in the totally remodeled home on our farm.

An Unusual Day

On one particular week in June 1983, Al rose early Monday morning as usual, quietly dressed so as not to totally awaken me, leaned over and kissed me on my cheek, whispered, "I love you," and left to drive to an oil well he was completing around Borger, Texas.

Throughout each day he was gone, he would always call several times on his mobile phone just to check in and make sure everything was OK. Then during each night, we would talk until he was so tired that I had to tell him to go to sleep. I loved those calls. It was as though he was taking care of me even though he was many miles away.

This week was unusual, however, because Al was supposed to return by noon on Thursday in time to meet with the crew that was going to start harvesting the wheat on our farm. Brynda and I had an appointment in Edmond, Oklahoma, at noon that Thursday to attend a luncheon and style show at Ruth Myers, an upscale dress shop for women. We were also going to meet with a woman who was interested in purchasing Brynda's dress shop in Kingfisher. As usual, the luncheon and style show were enjoyable, and Brynda and I critiqued every outfit in the show, determining if any could be right for us, and of course, several were.

Around 1:00, out of nowhere, a deep sense of foreboding quickly came over me. I tried to reject it and continue with the style show, but I could not shake that feeling. In those days, no one had cell phones so I excused myself and went into the back office to use their phone to see if I could reach Al. He had a mobile phone in his car but he did not answer, so I thought by this time he was probably at our farm away from his car and with the harvesters. I called my daughter Sandi's phone at the farm, and she answered on the first ring.

"Oh, Mom," she said breathlessly, "I thought this might be Dad."

"Have you not heard from him?" I asked.

"No," she said, "not a word, and the harvesters are here."

I assured her he would be there, "But don't let them start until he arrives. He wants to talk to them first."

"I know," Sandi insisted.

"Sandi, have him call me here at Ruth Myers as soon as he arrives."

She assured me she would so I hung up the phone and returned to my table at the luncheon, and Brynda asked softly, "Everything OK?"

"Yes, but your dad is running late, and the harvesters are waiting for him to get there so they can get started." I whispered.

"They can wait," Brynda responded, "Dad is paying them by the hour."

I once again tried to sit still and shake off the feeling of foreboding. My mind was filled with the fact of Al being late. He was never late without calling, but I thought to myself, *He is probably delayed in Borger and isn't able to call for some reason.* I kept assuring myself that he would be there any moment.

Another few minutes passed before I made another trip to the phone. "Sandi, is your dad there? Have you heard from him?"

"No Mom. Not a word."

When I returned to the table this time, I knew I could not stay another minute, and said to Brynda softly but firmly, "We've got to go!"

I Knew Something Was Wrong

The deep sense of foreboding would not let go. Something was wrong. I could feel it. We excused ourselves and immediately made our way to our car. I kept assuring myself everything would be fine and attempted to make myself be calm, but to no avail. The trip from Edmond back to Kingfisher is along dangerous back roads, and it seemed as though we were traveling in slow motion. Brynda was driving, and despite the poor roads, I turned to her and said, "Drive fast Brynda, drive fast!" And she did.

We entered Kingfisher heading west, and turned south on Main Street. As we approached the house, I fully expected to see Al's car parked in his normal spot, but it wasn't there. As Brynda drove into our driveway, I opened the door and started to get out before the car stopped.

"Be careful Mom," she said as she reached out to take my arm.

"I will, I will," I replied. "Call you later!" I shouted, shutting the car door as she drove away.

I kept telling myself that Al was at the farm with the harvesters, and he and Sandi had simply failed to call. If this was the case, I was certain he would have stopped by the house and changed his clothes before heading to the farm. Therefore, his oil field clothes would be in the utility room along with his work boots. My hands were shaking as I struggled to get the key in the lock to open the door. As I looked in the utility room, there was nothing there—no dirty clothes, no work boots—nothing!

I immediately grabbed the phone and called Sandi. "Sandi, is your dad at the farm?" I asked, holding my breath.

"No Mom, he's not here, and he has not called."

I tried to call his mobile phone in his car again. As the phone rang, I looked out the back door of our house across the large wooden deck and our pool when Gene and Betty Harris, our good friends, came walking up the stairs toward the door. I thought to myself, *Why in the world are they here?* I hung up the phone, opened the door and said, "Well, hello you two. What are you doing here?"

Betty was nervously wringing her hands as Gene said, "Marilyn, you need to come with us."

"I can't go anywhere," I replied. "I'm waiting for Al. He will be here at any moment."

He repeated, "Marilyn, you need to go with us."

I looked at him in absolute disbelief as though to say, "Did you not hear me? I cannot leave."

Then he said softly, "Marilyn, Al has been in an accident, and we've come to take you to him."

"Do you know where he is?" I asked abruptly. "Is there a problem, is he all right?"

"He has been in an accident. He is in the hospital in Okarche," he answered. Okarche was a small town 10 miles south of Kingfisher with a small community hospital.

"Have you seen him? Is he OK? Is he dead," I shouted?

"Just come go with us. We will take you to him," he insisted.

Finally, I obeyed. I dropped everything in my hands except my keys, and almost ran to my car.

"I'll drive, Marilyn. You sit up front with me," Gene insisted.

Betty got in the back, and we drove south on Highway 81 to Okarche, Oklahoma. I was numb; not a word was said among the three of us. About halfway to Okarche, our attorney and neighbor, Ron Phelps, was driving north on 81 to Kingfisher. When he spotted my red Mercedes, he blinked his lights and signaled to Gene to pull off the highway and stop. Ron turned around and drove up behind my car. I quickly jumped out of the car and ran back toward Ron, who had left his car and was coming toward me.

As I approached him, he took both of my hands in his hands, but did not speak. I looked him right in the eyes and said pleadingly, "Have you seen Al? Have you been with him? Is he OK?"

"He is dead!" was his only response.

Immediately, I threw his hands away from mine. I did not want to be touched.

"Have you seen his body?" I demanded. "Can you take me to him?"

"The best thing for you to do right now is to go back home. You can see him later," Ron insisted.

When he said that, I raised my fists to the sky and screamed at the top of my voice, "God, how dare You do this to me?" and slammed my fists across the trunk of the car, and began to weep bitterly!

Ron did not know what to do, so he simply stood still as I cried and pounded on the trunk. Finally, Ron asked, "Do you want to ride with me or go back to the house with Gene and Betty?"

I did not answer, but turned slowly and walked back to the front seat of my car with Gene and Betty, stopped crying and sat silently as Gene turned around and headed back to Kingfisher.

THE TARGET

CHAPTER 2

COMING TO GRIPS WITH THE DEATH OF MY LOVE

The short seven-minute drive back to my house was in absolute silence. I did not say a word, and Gene and Betty did not know what to say. By the time we arrived back at my house, a few people were already gathering. When I walked in the back door, I could smell the coffee brewing and saw several of my friends gathered in the kitchen. One well-meaning woman put her arm around me and quietly said, "It's wonderful to think that Al is in heaven and will be there waiting for you."

I looked at her in total disbelief, and wanted to slap her face, but simply walked away. Thankfully, no one else said a word; they simply looked and nodded their love and sorrow. I could feel their concern for me.

I made my way through our large, well-appointed kitchen, past the inner foyer with the magnificent old stairs and into the living room. I loved our living room. It was a large rectangular room which stretched across the entire front of the house. On two sides, there were large glass doors looking out on a front porch that mirrored the size of the room. The space was filled with beautiful furnishings which I had painstakingly chosen to give the room a feeling of elegance and warmth. My favorite was a large beautifully quilted sectional with a light cream background covered with pink and pale blue roses framed with green ivory vines. I placed it at the south end of the room in front of the windows. The northern portion of the room was dominated by a large fireplace framed by matching glassed-in bookshelves on each side. Love seats of quilted ivory with pale pink roses sat facing one another in front of the fireplace, along with an antique marble coffee table and end tables. They were the first tables Al and I bought after we married. Large crystal chandeliers hung at each end of this magnificent room which was the heart of our house. I loved it!

As I entered the room, several men were huddled about the room softly talking. They all stopped, looked at me and watched to see what I would do. I made my way across the room and sat down on the east end of my favorite couch near the front window. Once again, no one talked. They let me sit and be alone with my thoughts.

Help Me!

The living room had been the place of so many hours of pleasure for us. Al and I loved opening our home to our friends, and as a result, the old house was the site of major holiday gatherings each year, of which my favorite was Christmas. Christmastime was a celebration of joy at our house. Parties were filled with our closest friends from across the social and financial spectrum: oil executives, bankers, farmers, lawyers and scores of friends from our church came for the celebrations.

In order to accommodate our friends, our home was completely rearranged for the parties. Our dining room was connected to the living room through large envelope doors. At the center of the room was a massive gold leaf table with twelve matching chairs. For our Christmas party, we moved the chairs throughout the house and filled the table with the largest feast of holiday foods one could imagine. The soda fountain in the den served Christmas punch and became a gathering site throughout the party. Music from the antique radio filled the house with Christmas favorites. It was wonderful!

Yet, as I sat in the living room that day, I knew the celebrations would never return. Life would never be the same again. Sadness began to set in and overwhelm me. When I focused again on the room, my attention turned to the fireplace with its beautiful stonework and large wood mantle covering the north wall. Along the mantle were pictures and mementos of a life that had been so wonderful and was now over—cut short so quickly and unexpectedly. I could hardly breathe; the pain was so great.

As my eyes examined the mantle and stopped to reflect on each item, I noticed that the portrait of Al that an artist had painted was missing from its normal place on the mantel. *Where was it? Who had moved it? What happened to this special portrait?* Then suddenly I saw it! Someone had placed it on the floor with the face turned toward the wall. I stared down at it and studied the back of the frame and the missing picture. I could not move my eyes from the back of that empty canvas. My heart was screaming, "Help me! Help me!"

Once again, I silently shouted my question, "God, how dare You do this to me? Where were You when I needed You? Where were You when that truck headed straight toward Al?" My pain was greater than I could bear! I was lost in questions I could not answer and from which I could not escape. Over and over, my mind was screaming, "God, how dare You do this to me? I trusted You!"

I sat alone on the couch, lost in my thoughts. After a few moments, our banker's wife, Rene Cowell, came to the couch and sat down next to me, but she did not touch me. She just sat quietly and without saying a word. She just loved on me and grieved with me.

Where Is the Portrait?

As the crowd grew, only whispers filled the room, each person being more respectful than the last. In many ways, I was completely detached from the moment. My emotions were on absolute overload. My mind was racing with a thousand conflicting thoughts, *Why are all these people here? I want them to leave! Al will be home soon and I must prepare dinner. No, he is not coming! Someone told me he was dead, but that's a lie of the devil. Al is not dead! He can't be dead! I'm feeling faint!*

Ultimately, Brynda entered the living room and joined me on the sofa. Unbeknownst to me, my good friend, Vicki, the wife of our attorney, had gone to the home of my son, Steve, to tell him about the death of his father. The two of them drove to Brynda's home in order to share the news of her father's death, and traveled to the hospital in Okarche where his body had been taken. (For 20 years, I had no idea that Brynda was the only one of our family to see Al's body.) When they arrived at the hospital, Steve could not go in to identify his father's body, but Brynda did.

Now, Brynda was sitting next to me in a state of shock, holding me and softly crying as she repeatedly whispered, "This cannot be happening. This cannot be happening." We sat there for some time, simply holding one another in silence. After a while, she also noticed the missing portrait of Al and enquired, "Who moved Dad's portrait?" It wasn't until later that we learned that two of our friends had lovingly placed the painting on the floor next to the fireplace, thinking it would make it easier on us. But they were wrong!

Brynda ultimately left my side to assist Gene Harris as he went through our directory of friends and family to call them and break the terrible news of Al's death. I was still dry-eyed, wondering at times what all the fuss was about!

Dear God, This Can't be True!

Repeatedly, my eyes scanned the room, only to return to the fireplace, when I caught a glimpse of a young man on the front porch. It was my son, Steve. He was with a longtime friend, Robin Blair, standing by one of the thick wooden pillars that supported the balcony covering the porch. He would spend most of the next few days on the porch standing away from the crowd, lost in his thoughts. He looked like a little boy who has lost his most prized possession. And he had!

After about an hour of silence—alone in my thoughts—I left the solitude of the sofa and moved into the inner hallway next to the stately old staircase. It was there that I began to talk with some friends and allowed them to speak to me. No one really knew what to say. Several whispered, "I'm so sorry," and gave me loving hugs.

As I stood in the hallway quietly speaking with several of my dearest friends, I heard deep, wailing cries that sounded like an injured animal coming from the back porch. I instantly knew it was my youngest daughter, Sandi. She was totally distraught and could not stop crying. She threw open the door and quickly made her way through the crowded kitchen straight to me. Throwing her arms around me, she continued to sob the deepest, most painful sounds I have ever heard. Grabbing my arms and staring straight in my eyes, she screamed, "No mother, no, no, no. He can't be dead! He can't be dead!" I thought, *Dear God, this must be true!* My mind, my heart, my very soul was ebbing away. What if this is true?

Our hearts were breaking! We stood motionless—as priceless statues of grief—as others watched, but were afraid to touch. Sandi's husband, Brett, stood speechless at her side. After several minutes, he placed his arm around her and gently helped her to a chair, where she sat and continued to cry.

Throughout the evening, family friends from our town and those who worked with Al in the oilfield, came to the house. His death was such a tragic shock to scores of individuals that they simply had to come and be present. Many of them were dear friends who had been in our home scores of times, while others had never been in the house. But that night, due to the uniqueness of Al's life and the impact he had on those he met, they were there. Scores came—the wealthy, the poor, the powerful, the lowly, owners of oil companies and young roustabouts. They all came!

Several never said a word to me or the family, or in many cases to anyone else; they just came and stood for a few moments and quietly left. Within an hour or two of the accident, our house began to fill with flowers, dozens of bouquets and plants. Food started coming to the house. Grocery stores and individuals brought food and offered to help. The outpouring of love and concern was amazing!

Slowly but surely, my mind began to comprehend the hideous fact that my precious husband would never walk through the door again. I wondered, *God, where were You?*

As the day slowly passed, my closest friends insisted that I eat, but I couldn't. Toni Pickle, Sherry Blair and Betty Harris, all longtime friends of ours, were constantly working to keep food on the table for everyone. Renee Cowell, my friend and wife of our banker, brought me a small plate of food. She knew I had refused to eat, but she said softly, "Marilyn, if you will just eat two grapes, I won't ask you to eat anything else." I looked into her gently smiling face and said, "OK," as I took the two small green grapes. As I ate them, I wondered, *How long can I hold up?*

God, Where Were You?

Late that night when my mother and father arrived, I faced one of my greatest emotional challenges of the day. Both of my parents genuinely loved Al so much. With the loss of his parents many years earlier, he adopted my mother and father as his own, loved them deeply and genuinely cared for them.

When they entered my home that tragic night, they needed my support more than anyone else. My mother could not stop crying, and kept saying, "What will we do without him? What will we do; what will we do?" Through her tears, she said, "I was afraid something like this would happen since he had to drive so much." She desperately tried not to totally break down to keep my dad from breaking down, but she couldn't stop crying! All I could do was hold her. For some reason, as I held my mother, the fact that Al was truly gone broke over me. The pain was unbearable, as a reoccurring thought haunted me, *God, where were You!*

I had always tied Al's love and care for his parents and mine to divine protection over his life. He had been in many accidents, yet always survived. Many nights as I sat in the dark watching out the windows of my study for Al to return from a drilling rig, my heart would be pounding as I feared the worst. Then I would remember the scripture, "Honour thy father and thy mother: that thy days may be long upon the land which the Lord thy God giveth thee" (Exodus 20:12). So I constantly assured myself that Al would be protected because of how he loved our parents. No one could possibly honor his parents more than Al did his and mine. As I stood in the kitchen holding my mother, I thought again of that promise. Yet he had been killed. My faith was under attack!

The day had been very long and absolutely emotionally draining. My friends encouraged me again and again to go to bed and get some rest, but I did not want to go to my bedroom. It was our room. How could I stay in that room and sleep in that bed without him?

We got married during my senior year in high school and spent many years together. Our bedroom was our sanctuary. It was where we talked through every challenge we faced—some very painful, some very joyful. Like every marriage at this stage, we had settled into a wonderful life, rejoiced in each victory and enjoyed the sheer delight of being together.

I could not go into that room. Finally though, my exhaustion overran my emotional reservation, and I retired to my bedroom around 3:00 a.m. As always, I quickly bathed, brushed my hair, turned out the lights in my bathroom, and walked to my bed. I was startled as I pulled back the covers. Someone was in Al's side of my bed. For a split second, my heart pounded! *Maybe this was all a bad dream!* I flipped on the lamp and saw it was

Brynda. As only Brynda could, she would sleep with me for several months—and I needed it.

When I finally got into the bed, Brynda was asleep. I expected to be asleep in a few minutes too, but I was wrong. Despite taking the sleeping pills which would enable me to sleep all night, I did not sleep. Rather, the question I had shouted to God on the highway earlier returned, and I could not stop asking it again and again, "God, how dare You do this to me?" "Where were You?" I wanted to go out on the balcony and start screaming at God, "How could this happen? How dare You?"

After about an hour of trying to sleep and not being able to stop repeating that question, for some reason, I began to question the question. Why would I have said those words, in that way? Why did Al's death seem so unfair? After all, many people are killed in auto accidents. I always knew it was a possibility as much as he traveled, but I never dreamed it could happen to him.

CHAPTER 3

THE FIRST DAY ALONE

Our master bedroom suite was upstairs in a beautiful corner room. Large windows dominated the south wall, and antique glass doors opened to the balcony on the east. Sunlight filled the room throughout the day. In order to darken the room, I placed thick ceiling-to-floor drapes that completely blocked the light away from our bed. I always closed the drapes each night to ensure the sun would not wake us at dawn. However, the night of Al's death, I was so exhausted that I failed to fully close them. So, as one would expect on a bright and early June summer morning, the sun entered the room and interrupted what little sleep I had achieved that tragic night.

As I gradually awoke, I could smell coffee brewing in the kitchen, and for a fleeting moment, I thought Al was preparing coffee as he so often did. But quickly, the reality that Al was gone, returned. I wanted to pull the covers back over my head and disappear. *How would I go forward? What would my life be like without Al?*

Thankfully, Al had prepared for us financially, and for that I was deeply thankful. Our assets were safe. I would not lose my home or be forced to live without adequate funds. But I still wondered how I would live without him.

As I lay in bed, I heard voices coming from the kitchen and knew I had to go down and face the day. Slowly, I made my way to my bathroom to brush my hair, find my robe and make my way downstairs to wonderful friends who filled my kitchen. We had been together for many years and had shared every detail of our lives, but somehow death had not touched us. None of us were prepared for this tragedy; none of us knew how to respond. In some ways, I felt for our friends. They wanted desperately to comfort me, but at the same time, were hesitant to be too demanding with their concern. One thing was certain. They were determined that I would eat!

"Marilyn," they insisted, "you must eat. You have a long day in front of you, and you cannot go without food."

Hesitantly, I took the chair they reserved for me at the long bar in my kitchen, but could still not bring myself to eat. I sipped on my cup of coffee as I had gentle conversation with my precious friends. Their care for me began that morning and lasted for months. I could not have made it without them.

I Know Exactly What I Want

Midmorning, Brynda came into the kitchen and informed me that the funeral director had called and needed us to bring the clothes we wanted Al to wear. We both excused ourselves, and as we made our way upstairs, I thought to myself that this would be the last time I would ever dress him. (I had dressed him throughout our marriage for every special event.)

Brynda softly asked, "Do you have any idea what you want Dad to wear?"

"Yes," I replied, "I know exactly what I want."

A few weeks earlier, I had purchased a beautiful dark blue sports coat for him. He looked great in it! The coat was distinguished and dressy, yet casual enough that he could wear it proudly. He had scores of slacks, but I had bought a light gray pair to go with the coat—never thinking they would serve as his burial clothes. I found a freshly laundered white dress shirt, and Brynda insisted on a red tie. Once we laid his clothes out on the bed, she said, "Mom, he must be buried in his new black Ostrich cowboy boots." I agreed. Then we placed the clothes in a travel bag and gave them to Steve because he wanted to take his clothes to the funeral home and make the final decision on the casket.

Al, Al, Al, What Have You Done?

Brynda received a call from our pastor who informed us that he would pick us up around noon to go to the funeral home to view

Al's body. Keith Maule was the pastor of the Nazarene Church in Kingfisher—our family pastor and a man deeply loved by Al. It was only fitting that he would drive my daughters and me to Guthrie to view Al's body and complete the final funeral arrangements.

The 30-minute trip to Guthrie was somber. Pastor Keith asked a few questions to break the heaviness of the moment, but for the most part we were all caught up in the silence of our individual grief and bewilderment.

When we arrived at the Davis Funeral Home in Guthrie, Mr. Davis met us as we approached the door of the facility and ushered us into the family room. After a few moments of greetings, he asked if we were prepared to view the body and then proceeded to take us back to the viewing room. Before he opened the casket, Mr. Davis turned to me and said, "Mrs. Wheeler, we have done the best we could with everything, but the left side of his head was very seriously wounded and it was difficult to totally cover. I hope you will be pleased."

Had he not told me of the problems with the wound, I probably wouldn't have noticed; but when he opened the casket, the first thing I saw was the wound. As my daughters and I stood transfixed in front of the casket for several minutes, tears filled my eyes as I looked upon the wonderful face of the one I loved, and the one who loved me, and cared so deeply for me and our little family. I finally focused on his closed eyes and whispered, "Al, Al, Al, what have you done?"

At that moment, all pretenses were over. It was real. My precious husband was dead. Pastor Keith moved to my side and gently said, "Remember Marilyn, Al is not here. This is just his body."

I knew that and believed it, but I needed to hear it again. His words brought amazing comfort to me and for the first time since the accident, the fact that Al was with the Lord Jesus—whom he loved—became real. We stood in front of his casket for nearly an hour. We cried, prayed, cried, laughed and cried again as we rejoiced that we had known him and the love he had for each of us. We had been wonderfully blessed!

Brynda placed two peppermints in his inside coat pocket because he never went to church without peppermints for the pastor's son. Sandi had written a letter to her dad and placed it in the casket. Finally, we returned to Pastor Keith's car and made our way back to Kingfisher.

The Final Sign

Our home had been the gathering place for a group of young men and women to study the Bible and pray each week since 1978. Al and I led this band of young zealots, many of whom are in the ministry today. One of the most committed was Ellis Weber, who also worked in the oil field, but was really a radical Christian committed to changing the world. He even pastored a new church filled with young believers in Kingfisher. He was close friends with our children, especially Brynda and Sandi, who were themselves extremely committed to the Lord Jesus. As soon as Ellis heard of Al's death, he came to our home. He also wrote a tribute to Al that was published in our local paper. It was so beautiful and accurate.

That afternoon slowly passed for me as more and more people came to share their love and grief with us. My sleeplessness the night before ultimately caught up to me and I was forced to take leave for a rare afternoon nap.

As I napped, my children grew more and more restless with the unfairness of their father's death. Brynda was convinced that they should return to Guthrie and raise Al from the dead. Al taught our family to believe big! Meeting with Ellis and Sandi, Brynda insisted, "If any of us were dead, Dad would at least try to bring us back to life!" They all agreed.

The decision to attempt to raise Al from the dead was finally made late Friday night. I refused to let them go without me, even though I told them I did not have faith to pray for Al to be raised from the dead. They understood and agreed that I should go with them. Brynda; Sandi and her husband, Brett; Ellis; and I loaded into his car right after midnight to make the 30-minute trip back to Guthrie. The trip was filled with prayers and encouraging one another to have confidence in the success of their effort. I kept my mouth shut and did not say a word because I did not have their level of faith.

The funeral home was dark; even the porch light was out. Obviously, the Davis' were asleep. That did not deter us. The five of us walked up the steps of the porch and boldly knocked on the door around 1:00 a.m. Finally, Mrs. Davis opened the door, dressed in her housecoat, looked at me and said, "Mrs. Wheeler, is everything all right? May I help you?"

I replied, "Please excuse us, I know this is strange, but my children want to see their father."

"No, no, no," she answered, "nothing is strange around here. Please come in." She graciously escorted us back toward the viewing room and asked us to give her time to prepare the casket. In just a few moments, she opened the door of the room and invited us in. When she did, Ellis informed her we had come to take Al home. She looked at me, and I shook my head to remove her concern.

I told the others I did not want my lack of faith to stand in the way so I chose to wait in the hallway outside the viewing room. My concern was for them; I did not want their faith or their confidence in the Lord Jesus to be hurt. My prayer that night was for them more than for the resurrection of Al (although the resurrection would have been stupendous!).

Brynda, Sandi, Brett and Ellis entered the room and stood around the casket, singing and praying for several minutes. They asked the Lord to either raise Al from the dead or give them a clear sign that he was where he wanted to be and they needed to accept his death. While Ellis prayed, the others laid their hands on his body and demanded death to leave and his life return.

As they prayed, Brynda noticed that a small amount of blood began to trickle from the side of his mouth, and called its attention to the others. She took a tissue and blotted the blood, but it quickly returned. At first, they ignored the blood, but ultimately, each of them believed the blood leaving his body was a sign that his death was certain, and they needed to accept the fact. Their prayers for resurrection turned to prayers of rejoicing, and they praised the Lord Jesus for the time they had had with him, and committed themselves to staying faithful in the future.

Our trip back home was somber. Each of us was individually dealing with the finality of his death differently. It was as though we took turns crying and riding in silence. When we arrived home around 2:00 a.m., Brynda showed me the blood she had wiped from the side of Al's mouth. "Mom, look at this."

"What is that?" I asked.

"It is blood that came from Dad's mouth," she replied. "It's a sign! Life is in the blood. When I saw the blood leaving his body, I knew life had departed, and we must accept it. That's all I needed to know."

CHAPTER 4

I MET HER IN A COTTON PATCH

I exhaustively made it to bed around 2:30 a.m., thinking there was no way I could stay awake. But I was wrong. As I lay in bed, hoping to sleep, I began to think past the death of my precious husband to our early days together and how through all our experiences, I saw him grow into a great man of faith with absolute confidence in the love and power of the Lord Jesus Christ.

Al and I both grew up on small farms in southwest Oklahoma, less than 10 miles apart, yet we never really met until I was 16. However, I first saw him when I was only 10, and thought he was the best looking guy in the world.

Every year my Dad, who was a farmer and rancher, wanted to help my brothers have a little job and income of their own.

When my oldest brother, Bill, was about 12, my dad planted him a small cotton patch—just a few acres. When the cotton was ready to be picked, Bill would get our two younger brothers to help him pick the cotton.

One day when I was 10 years old or so, it was forecasted to rain, so Bill asked me if I would help them get the cotton in. He said he would pay me what the cotton gin was paying him— about 2 cents a pound, I believe. So, always looking for extra quarters, I said I would do it. We picked cotton that afternoon and stopped awhile to watch as an oilfield drilling rig moved in right next to our cotton patch. My brothers and I watched the young men hoist the floor of the rig up and lay down the pipe. As it was getting dark, we left the rig site and walked the small distance to our house.

The next day, my brothers and I went to the cotton patch to finish picking the cotton. When we got there, we were surprised to find a huge pile of picked cotton stacked up right in the middle of the field! We all looked at each other in amazement; then my brother Bill, who has always been good at making money and could think on his feet, said "This is my cotton. I came here last night and picked it." Not to be outdone, my younger brother Ronnie said "No, you didn't, I picked it early this morning!" So, the squabble began.

Then a handsome young guy, who looked every bit of 15 or 16, left the drilling rig and came to settle the argument (which was getting a little bit out of hand). He said, "Hey guys, we had to put this guide line wire down in your cotton patch to help hold the rig up. I didn't want to destroy your cotton, so I just picked it for you, and I want the little girl to have it." I was delighted; I thought he was very cute, and dreamed about him for days! Little did I know at the time that this generous young man would become my husband someday!

It was six years before I saw him again. But when I look back now, I can see the Lord Jesus was at work in both of our lives, preparing us for our life together and for the unique experiences we would have as Christians.

Granny and Grandpa

My family and I lived on a farm about a mile and a half from town. Our house was an unusually large farm house with enough space for my mother and father, four growing boys and me. Our family attended church every time the doors were opened, and like many churches in small towns in those days, most of the men in our community thought church was for women and children, so they hung out on the car fenders of the cars or church steps. That is where my dad was during most church services. I always wanted him to come inside, but he rarely did. Later in life, he would attend church with Mom and actually became a quiet, reserved Christian.

I was blessed to have powerful, godly women in my life, including my mother, aunt and grandmother. My best friend was my cousin, Carolyn. She was the daughter of my mother's twin sister, my closest companion and the "sister" I never had. Carolyn and I were inseparable. We went to school together, attended the same church, and saw each other almost every day.

Like most girls from our small town, our teen years were filled with talks about boys and shared dreams of being married and having children.

Being the only girl in a family of five children, I was the privileged one. My four brothers almost never went to Granny's to spend the night—but I did! Throughout my teen years, I spent most weekends and holidays at her house. She was very precious to me. She and my grandfather lived in a special country home that sat next to the major highway going through the small town we all loved and also the house in which I was born. She was known as "Aunt Dora" to friends and neighbors, but she was "Granny" to me and all her 22 grandkids.

I loved being with Granny as she was so spiritual, yet so practical. She taught me to love the Lord Jesus and trust Him totally. On Saturdays, we would go to "town." Town was Cement, Oklahoma, a small place of 500 residents.

Grandma was a lively, tall, slender lady who loved to dress up and go to church. She and I walked about twelve blocks to church each Sunday, and then someone would give us a ride home. I enjoyed the walk since it gave us the chance to talk about all the things going on in everybody's life—as much as we knew anyway. Granny said we must never gossip—just have conversations.

Now, Grandpa was a totally unique man with a mind of his own and very few words, unless you got him talking. He always acknowledged me being present in his house, but he just left the girls to themselves. He was a retired blacksmith who had shoed many horses in his day (allegedly horses belonging to some boys by the name of "Floyd"—Pretty Boy, I think it was, and the James Boys and Dalton Brothers).

Grandpa could spin the tales when he was in a talking mood, and we lapped up every word. He told us about the night my mother and her twin sister were born. They were so small that they slept in shoe boxes set on the coal stove (open) oven door like a warm incubator. As they grew, they shared a dresser drawer, all lined in soft fur and flannel, as they were January babies and needed the warmth.

My mother and her sister shared many stories of their childhood with me. I especially remember the one of a distant cousin, Cynthia Ann, the young white girl captured by the Apache Indians who ultimately became the mother of the great Apache chief, Quanah Parker.

I Can't Get Married in These Shoes

Life changed when I entered high school. I was finally allowed to date at the age of 16. Growing up in a small town and attending a tiny school, you pretty much knew everyone. It was always interesting to see who started dating whom. One of my best friends, Barbara Wainscott, was dating Perry Sutterfield, the Baptist pastor's son. Perry's best friend was George Johnston, who was a great baseball player and received a scholarship to play baseball at OSU, so Barbara arranged a double date for George and me to go out with Perry and her. We dated for nearly two years.

One night, the four of us were together and we talked about running off to Texas to get married. Barbara turned to me and excitedly asked, "Is that good with you, Marilyn?"

I replied, "I guess so." But then I remembered I had on the wrong shoes, and said, "I can't get married in these shoes." Needless to say, our plans for eloping that day were canceled.

On another occasion, the four of us arranged to double date and attended a birthday party held at Isabelle Scott's home. About 30 high school kids were there. As the party progressed, I noticed a young man I did not know. I thought he was the best looking guy I had ever seen. He was about 5 feet 10 inches with beautiful olive skin, black wavy hair and big brown eyes. He was well-built with strong muscular arms, and seemed more mature than the others. He looked familiar, but I knew I had never met him before.

At one point, we were playing Spin the Bottle. If the boy's bottle pointed at a girl, the two were to walk around the outside of the house together. Speaking of the stranger with the wavy black hair, I told Barbara, "If he tries anything with me, I will slap his face!"

I noticed as couples came back from walking around the house they were usually holding hands. Finally, the bottle of the stranger landed on me. So, I obeyed. I introduced myself and he told me his name was Al. We began slowly walking around the house. I could see why couples were holding hands going around the house; it was dark and very hard to keep your balance. But Al never offered to help and certainly never held my hand. As we were walking around the house, Al jokingly said, "Are you here with your brother?"

"No!" I snapped, "he is my boyfriend."

Al responded as though he was the older and wiser, "You're much too young to have a boyfriend and be dating by yourself." About that time, we arrived back at the front of the house, and I quickly made my way to George.

277 Diner

My parents allowed me to take an after-school job at the local 277 Diner as a waitress. We wore cute uniforms with aprons that tied in the back. Following our encounter of walking around the house at the birthday party, Al began coming to the diner on a regular basis. The first time he was there, I was standing with my back to him waiting on another table, when he reached up and untied my apron strings. When he did that, the apron fell to the floor and I almost tripped. I turned to him and said, "What on earth are you doing?"

He grinned and quipped, "Trying to get some attention." And he did! From that point forward, he was in the diner around closing time on a regular basis—and I looked forward to his being there! We had an easy time talking to each other, and as we talked, the conversations grew more and more serious. I could feel myself falling for him, and I could tell he felt the same way about me.

I usually got off work every night around 10 o'clock, so my dad would come and wait for me to finish and drive me home. One night when Al was in the diner, he noticed my dad waiting for me. "Is that your dad?" he asked.

I nodded my head, yes, and he left the diner and went out to my dad's car and spoke with him. This went on for several nights.

One Friday night as my shift ended, my dad was not there to pick me up. Al offered to take me home. "Oh no," I said, "my dad will be here any minute."

"No!" he replied with a little smile, "I asked him if I could drive you home, and he agreed."

I shrugged my shoulders and walked to his car. From that night, this scenario became a regular routine—and I enjoyed it more and more.

A New Wristwatch

My boyfriend, George, was in Stillwater, Oklahoma, playing baseball at OSU. He only came home on a few weekends and during the summer, he was busy making money for college expenses, so we spent very little time together.

On my seventeenth birthday, George gave me a beautiful new wrist watch. I was so excited! I wore it to work the next day, and as always, Al appeared at closing time to drive me home. "Is that a new watch?" he asked.

"Yes. I got it for my birthday from George." I replied and proudly showed it to him.

"It's alright," he muttered.

The next day when Al showed up at the diner, he had a small beautifully gift-wrapped package in his hand. When I opened it, of course, it was a watch several times more expensive than the one George had given me. "Thank you so much!" I exclaimed, as I put Al's watch on my other arm. But he was not pleased.

This could only go on for so long. Finally, George asked me if I was seeing someone else. "I know that dark haired grease monkey likes you," he said sarcastically. ("Grease-monkey" was the insulting name used to describe young men who worked on the oil wells.)

I admitted to George that I was seeing Al and wanted to continue seeing him. Needless to say, that ended my relationship with George. After this, I wrote George a nice letter; he wrote me back, and we never spoke again for 25 years.

Dedicated to God

The following six months were like a whirlwind. Al and I began seriously dating in August before my senior year. I was a student in high school and working every evening at the 277 Diner. Al worked every day in the oil field. Despite our demanding schedules, we managed to see each other every night after I left work.

The business slowed at the diner toward the end of the evening so this gave us a chance to talk and get to know each other better. Al had thick black wavy hair which he usually wore tousled down across his forehead. As we were talking one evening, he reached up and brushed his hair back for a moment, and when he did, I noticed for the first time that he had horizontal scars stretching across his forehead. As he was fixing his hair back in place, I said, "Stop a minute, let me see your forehead."

"It's nothing," he replied.

"Well, let me see," I insisted.

He paused for a moment, then ran his fingers through his hair and pulled it away from this forehead.

"How did you get those scars?" I asked softly.

"I paid dearly for them. In fact, I almost died getting them," he said, smiling back at me.

"Tell me. Come on, tell me," I said, coaxing the answer from him.

"Seriously," he began, "I did almost die getting them. A few years ago, I was working on a rig with a friend of mine named Dick Short, who was both an oil field worker and a Pentecostal preacher. We were doing twelve hour shifts on a well near Weatherford, Oklahoma. When we got off work one night, we were both extremely tired, but decided to drive back home since we had the next day off. Dick was driving a company pickup and agreed to drop me off at my home outside Anadarko, Oklahoma.

It was a little after midnight, and we were both fighting off sleep, when we went around a curve heading south on highway

281. As we rounded the curve, out of nowhere a large oilfield service truck coming north toward us had drifted totally over into our lane. There was no way to avoid smashing head on into each other."

Al continued, "All I remember was a large crashing sound! When I woke up, I was lying on the ground covered in blood. Several of the arteries on my neck and head had been cut and my forehead was covered with lacerations. Dick was literally holding my scalp together and praying for me. He was seriously praying! He promised God that if I could live, I would love Him and serve Him the rest of my life."

Al hesitated and looked at me for some affirmation, and then he said, "I guess he dedicated me to God."

I paused for just a moment to catch my breath, and replied, "That's wonderful! Not that you got hurt, of course, but that Dick dedicated you to God."

From that point forward, every time I saw those scars, they reminded me that Al had faced death—and God had given him a new life. As we moved forward together, I returned again and again to the thought that God had protected his life, especially when he got hurt. As a result, I took the reoccurring injuries as simply something that happens, and nothing more.

Al faithfully drove me home from the diner night after night and was always a perfect gentleman. However, one night he stopped the car a couple of blocks from my house, put his arm around my shoulder and gently kissed me. I knew it was going to happen soon, and when it did, I was thrilled! It was that moment that I knew I loved him and wanted to spend the rest of my life with him.

Permission to Get Married

Al was an unusual young man. Although he was only twenty-two when we got married, he sometimes seemed much older. He was the sole support of his ailing parents when we met. He was one of thirteen children. He had six brothers and six sisters so he learned responsibility and caretaking way too young. He was the youngest boy, with two sisters younger than him, although they had both gotten married before we did. Al was left at home to care for his mother, who, when I met him, was dying of cancer.

As Christmas approached during my senior year, Al and I began to talk seriously about marriage. We both knew we were meant to be together as husband and wife. One day without me knowing, Al met with my dad to ask to marry me.

"Mr. Esmon?" Al started, "You know Marilyn and I've been spending a lot of time together, and I have fallen deeply in love with her."

Dad interrupted, "Well, I think she feels the same way about you."

"I think she does," Al continued, "and I hope your family does also."

Dad agreed, "We do. In fact, I can't find anything about you not to like. We appreciate that you are a hard worker, and the way you care for your mother and dad is admirable."

"Thank you, sir," Al replied. "I am here to ask you for your permission for me to marry your daughter as soon as you think we can."

Dad sighed a moment, and looking squarely into his eyes, he said, "Albert, you have my permission."

"Thank you, thank you, Mr. Esmon."

The following Friday was New Year's Day, and as usual, Al and I spent the evening together. When he drove me home, we stopped at our usual place to be alone for a few moments. As soon as he stopped, he turned toward me and said, "I've been wanting to ask you a question all evening."

"Really, what's that?" I asked.

He reached inside his shirt pocket and pulled out an engagement ring, and softly asked, "Will you marry me?"

"I think you know my answer," I said.

He nodded his head, and said, "I do, but I want it to be official."

"Yes," I replied, "I want very much to marry you, but you must ask my Dad."

A big smile broke out on his face, and he said with certainty, "I have!"

"You talked to Dad?" I asked.

"Yes I did, and he gave his permission," Al replied with a certain proud delight. At that moment, Al placed the ring on my finger and we were officially engaged. He put his strong arms around me, kissed me wonderfully—as we hugged and hugged. We were going to be married! Everything was perfect!

In those days, every young bride wanted a June wedding, and I was no different. Our plans were for us to be married as soon as I graduated from high school. I wanted Brother J. L. Stanridge, who was the pastor of the First Assembly of God Church in Cement, Oklahoma and our family pastor, to perform the marriage ceremony. When I approached him about the wedding later that week, he assured me he wanted to do so, but needed to meet my fiancé before he agreed.

When we met with Brother Stanridge, he discussed several issues and then asked Al if he had ever truly accepted Jesus as his Lord and Savior. Al told him he had been baptized, but had never really been saved. The pastor proceeded to ask him if he would like to receive Jesus, and Al said, "Yes, with all my heart!"

Brother Stanridge replied, "Good, let's pray right now and ask Jesus to save you and make you a Christian."

The pastor led Al in the prayer of salvation, and he received Jesus as his Lord and Savior. Then the pastor prayed a prayer of blessing over him. It was a precious time that forever changed his life. Al Wheeler was radically born again, and was never the same! From that point forward, Al loved God with all his heart and was not ashamed to share Jesus with anyone he could get to listen to him. It was the first step in what was to become a remarkable Christian life, filled with the supernatural power of the Holy Spirit.

We began our lives together as two young people who loved the Lord Jesus and each other. Through it all, Al never let me forget the cotton patch. He loved to laugh and make others laugh. I honestly don't remember a day when he wasn't smiling. One of his favorite moments occurred when someone would ask him how he met his wife. Al always said, "I found her in a cotton patch in Oklahoma." That would always irritate me when he said it—but it was true!

THE TARGET

CHAPTER 5

THE EARLY MOMENTS OF MARRIAGE

I was deeply in love and extremely excited about marrying Al. My mother and I immediately started planning for our June wedding. It was difficult to keep my mind on school even though I was vying to graduate at the top of my class. Every girl in school had to see my ring and hear me go on and on about my wonderful new fiancé. At the same time, Al was traveling back and forth to Texas—working in the oil field, and taking care of his ailing mother.

Each week, Al took his mother to Baylor Hospital in Texas for radiation to fight her cancer. After one particularly difficult radiation treatment the week before Valentine's Day, the doctors told him and his mother there was no reason for her to return for additional treatments. They had done all they could, and sadly told him that she had only a couple months to live.

On the way back to Oklahoma, Al's mother asked, "Albert, you know one thing I would like?"

"Anything Mother, whatever you want, I will do it!" Al replied.

Mrs. Wheeler leaned up in the car seat and asked, "Would you consider moving the date of your wedding up so I can see you married? I might not get to attend, but at least I would know my youngest son has a wife." Al was also the last of ten brothers and sisters to still be living at home. "I think I can Mom; I'm sure we can," he assured her.

When Al picked me up on Valentine's, I could tell he was troubled. He was quiet, and the normal wonderful smile was missing from his face.

"What's bothering you?" I asked.

"It's Mom," he replied. "She is extremely sick. I know I'm about to lose her."

"I'm so sorry," I said softly.

He looked at me with those big brown eyes and whispered, "Would you be terribly disappointed if we did not have a June wedding?"

"Are you wanting to call off the marriage?" I quickly asked.

"No, never," he responded, "I'm just wondering if we could get married before June."

"Why, what's going on?"

Then he turned to me and told me of his mother's wish to see her youngest son, and last child at home, marry before her death. I assured him we could work something out, but we must talk to my parents. We left immediately and sat down with them in the living room of my house.

Al led the conversation. "Mr. and Mrs. Esmon," he began, "my mother is very ill and will not live much longer. She told me there is one thing she wants before she dies. She wants to see me married, but to do so, we would need to move the wedding to an earlier date. May we have your permission to move the wedding forward?"

Dad and Mother looked at each other, and as always, mother said to Dad, "It's up to you."

We all sat in silence as Dad thought to himself for a moment. Then he looked directly at Al, and said, "Albert, I will give my permission under one condition. Marilyn must complete high school and graduate." Al gave my father his word that I would finish school and graduate with my class.

Then Dad moved his gaze to me and continued, "Marilyn, this will be a very different time for you. You will be a married woman. You will not be able to run around with your friends as usual. Albert will be traveling back and forth to Texas to work in the oil fields. You won't be able to go to Texas with him each week until school is out. Do you understand that?"

"Yes Daddy, I understand," I answered.

"Ok," he finished, "you have my permission to marry as soon as possible."

It was a moment of delight and a little apprehension. We immediately pulled out the calendar and took a serious look at when we could realistically have the wedding. It was Sunday night, Valentine's Day, February 14. Al had a job drilling an oil well in Texas, and the best time for his work schedule would be in two weeks.

"Two weeks?" I asked. "Can we be ready for a wedding in two weeks?" As we talked, we all decided we could. So, the decision was made that we would be married in 12 days on Friday night, February 26, 1954.

A Wedding in Two Weeks?

One of the immediate decisions was finding a place to live in two weeks. The postmaster in Cement was my friend. In our small town, people went to the post office to pick up the mail every day. As a result, she and I talked about every event in our lives. She had totally renovated the cutest little one-bedroom house for herself to live in when she retired. From the paint, to the carpet, to the appliances—everything about it was new. It was wonderful, almost like a doll house. When she heard of our marriage plans, she allowed us to rent her beautiful little house before she even lived in it herself.

Everything moved so fast that I did not have time to prepare for a splashy wedding, but I knew in my heart it was the right decision. My friends were excited for us, and everyone did what they could to help us prepare. In a small town, it is not difficult for everyone to be informed quickly and for arrangements to be made.

The day of our wedding was like all weddings…hectic and wonderful. I was so excited, I skipped school to prepare. Our small Assembly of God church was decorated with candles and flowers. My cousin, Carolyn, was my maid of honor, and two of my classmates, Nona Sites and Rolland Joe Webb, sang the song, "Always." Brother Stanridge preformed the ceremony and made it very personal. Our wedding was simple, yet very special.

Following the service, we could not escape a little hazing. The young men had prepared a wheel barrel for Al to push me in up and down Main Street. It was great fun. Our friends clapped, laughed and cheered as we made our way through the town. As soon as we returned to the church, Al and I left to go by our little house, grab our bags and depart Cement as husband and wife for a quick weekend honeymoon in Texas because I had to be back in school on Tuesday.

We got married on February 26, and Al's mother died on April 2. Al dearly loved his mother, and even though he knew she was with the Lord, took her passing very hard.

Oh My Gosh! I Forgot the Beans!

I graduated in May and immediately departed Cement to join Al at his work in Texas. One of the first lessons I learned about being married to an oil man was not to plan on living in any one place very long. When a young man is working in the oil field, his family must also move as they hunt for oil and gas. When the drilling rig moved out of Texas and into Oklahoma, Al and I had to follow. At this time, we had been married four months and were living in our third house—this time in Duncan, Oklahoma.

During our first summer together, I discovered firsthand the extent to which a young oil man must be away from home and at the rig. As a result, there were many lonely days and nights. To offset those moments, I quickly learned to make friends with my neighbors, and find a church in which I could be involved.

I was also learning to be a homemaker. Every homemaker must be able to decorate, and I was determined to decorate our little home and make it very special. My first project was a dining room set. I bought it for twenty dollars at a secondhand store. It was an old, scratched oak table with matching chairs. I loved the shape, but not the color. So, I repaired the scratches and painted it with black lacquer. Then I found beautiful red rose decals at the Ben Franklin store and placed them on the back of each chair. I thought it was wonderful!

My next step was learning to be a good cook. I had never cooked a full meal, but one afternoon, I decided to make a big pot of beans and ham. So I placed the big pan on the stove and set it to slowly cook so it would be prepared by the time Al came home. When he came in the door, he said, "Honey, let's go to the movie. The Ten Commandments is showing."

I was so excited to have time with my husband and to get out of the house that I hurriedly got dressed and left with him, totally forgetting the pot of beans cooking on the stove. The Ten Commandments lasted for at least three hours. When it was over, we headed for home. As we turned the corner on our block and got a glimpse of our house, we could see smoke pouring out of the front door.

"Oh my gosh," I shouted, "I forgot the beans!"

"The beans?" Al asked.

"Yes, I was cooking ham and beans for tonight," I cried.

At which, Al laughed and laughed. I did not think it was funny! When we arrived back home, our house was filled with firefighters and policemen, and Al could not stop laughing. He told the story of his new wife trying to burn down the house with a pot of beans to everyone he knew and met for the rest of his life.

Sure Enough, I Was Pregnant!

As we settled into our routine in Duncan, Oklahoma Al wanted to immediately start a family; but three months passed, and I was not pregnant. One morning, early in September, I was so sick—nauseous and vomiting. I thought I had picked up a simple stomach virus, but it did not stop. Morning after morning for nearly a month, the symptoms returned. I finally said to Al over breakfast, "I might be pregnant."

He was thrilled at the possibility, and responded, "Go to the doctor today and find out. If you are, we need to make sure everything is right so we can take perfect care of you."

My family doctor was in Cement and had retired. Now, I was in Duncan and had never needed a doctor. "It might be difficult to see a doctor today since I will be a new patient," I insisted.

"At least try," he responded.

I promised him I would see the doctor as soon as I could get an appointment. I went to the doctor and sure enough, I was pregnant, and had been for a month—which meant the baby would be born in May. I liked my Duncan doctor and committed myself to following his instructions, especially his demand that even though I only weighed 110 pounds, I was not to gain over 15 pounds during the pregnancy.

CHAPTER 6

THE ARMY CALLS

Fall passed with our regular routine of Al working and me pregnant and getting more pregnant every day. In December, an envelope arrived from the Draft Board in Al's home town of Anadarko, Oklahoma. He had received a deferment since he was the sole support of his ailing mother and father, but with her death, the deferment ended, and he was now eligible for the draft. That letter was quickly followed by another informing us that he was being drafted and was to report on Monday, January 3. Here I was four months pregnant and Al was leaving to serve in the army for two years. Thank God America was not at war! Yet our personal world had just turned upside down!

Al gave his notice to the drilling company in Duncan, and we moved back to Cement. On January 3, the Greyhound bus stopped in front of the 277 Diner, and Al boarded the bus to Ft.

Riley, Kansas along with six other draftees to begin serving two years in the army. As the bus drove away, we were all there—my Mom, Dad, and two of my brothers, along with several of my friends who were hugging, kissing and yelling at the top of our collective voices, "Goodbye, Al. We love you!"

Some men would have been embarrassed, but Al said he loved it, especially seeing his beautiful, young, blonde, pregnant wife crying, waving and throwing kisses to him.

When Al left, I returned to my parent's home and settled back into my room. Despite being a pregnant army wife, I enjoyed being with my high school friends in Cement. Since I had our car, I was free to go where I wanted, which included my grandma's house. I loved being with her again, and since the phone lines had not yet reached to our home in the country, I especially enjoyed her phone because I could speak to Al during the weekend.

One benefit of being an army wife was getting to go to the Reynolds Army Hospital at Fort Sill, Oklahoma, and doctors close to my home. My parents drove me to each of my doctor's appointment as I got closer and closer to giving birth to our first child. My doctor was a colonel, who was even more demanding about the dangers of weight gain in pregnancy. He threatened to hospitalize me if I gained over 15 pounds. I was so concerned about being overweight that I only ate boiled eggs and grapefruit on many days.

Steve Arrives Three Weeks Later

Finally May arrived! The doctors had told me the baby would be born around the first of May, but they were wrong. Three weeks later, my baby boy decided it was time to make an appearance. He could not have picked a more miserable day. Thursday the nineteenth started out as a rainy day early in the morning and did not stop. I went to the kitchen that rainy morning and said to my Mom, "I hope I don't go into labor today."

But I did.

That afternoon around 5:00 p.m., the pain started in earnest. I had everything prepared for the trip to the hospital at Ft. Sill which was an hour or more from my home. About 6 p.m., my parents, little brother and I made our way through pouring rain to the car. It was a miserable night and a scary drive through the water to the hospital. At times, my Dad drove through water up to the bottom of the car doors. Finally, we arrived at Ft. Sill, drove through the guard gate, and up the hill to Reynolds Army Hospital.

The people at Reynolds could not have been nicer. They immediately took me to my room on the third floor and then checked to see how far along I was. The nurse, who would be with me through the night, was very reassuring and said, "Well, young lady, you will probably be in labor for most of the night."

My mother agreed, "First babies can take hours to arrive!"

My parents had left two of my brothers at home alone, and I could tell my mother was concerned about them on a stormy

Oklahoma night. After staying with me for a couple hours, I insisted they go home. The nurse promised my parents that I would be fine. "She is very healthy and has great doctors and nurses watching over her."

"I'll be alright," I said encouraging them, "and will probably be right here in this room all night. Go home, and I'll see you tomorrow."

"We will be right back early in the morning," Mom responded. Dad leaned over, kissed me on the forehead and wiped away a tear. "I'll be thinking about you all night."

"I know Daddy. I'll be fine."

When they left, the reality of what was happening rushed over me for a moment. I was a teenager having my first baby, and at the moment, I was alone in a strange hospital. I quickly prayed, "Father, I know You are here with me, and I'm confident of Your love and protection. Thank You for blessing me."

As soon as I finished praying, I relaxed and settled back in my bed with genuine excitement at the birth of my first child. In about an hour, the contractions and pain seriously increased. Right after midnight, they took me to the delivery room and thankfully gave me a spinal block. The pushing began. Everything went well and in a short while, my precious son, Steven Albert Wheeler, entered the world at 8 pounds, 8 ounces. The nurses prepared me to return to my room, and I easily slept through the remainder of the night.

The next morning the nurses rolled a bassinet next to my bed and brought Steve to me. In an army hospital in those days, the baby stayed with the mother and the mother cared for the child if she was able. As they had promised, my parents arrived early and were thrilled with their new grandson. They spent the day with me, helping to care for Steve and giving me time to rest.

The Surprise Visitor at the Window

The biggest shock of my stay in the hospital came late that night. My parents had returned home, and Stevie and I were sleeping. I was awakened by the sound of noise coming from my window. Soon it sounded as though someone was knocking on the window. Since I was on the third floor of the hospital, I could not imagine what was taking place, and I was very concerned that the knocking was going to wake up Stevie. Since it would not stop, I finally got up from my bed to check the window to see if I could determine what was making the noise.

When I opened the curtains, I was startled! The moonlight was shining on a man standing on the fire escape right outside my window. For a moment, when I saw he was wearing a uniform and hat, I thought it was a policeman or fireman. Then, I realized, it was Al! "What on earth are you doing?" I asked through the window.

"Unlock the window!" he said, pointing up to the lock. When I unlocked the window, he raised it from the outside and crawled through. I have never been so hugged in my life. He kissed and kissed and kissed me. It was all sort of a blur.

Then I exploded with questions, "How did you get away from Ft. Riley? Why did you come through the window? Are you supposed to be here? What's going on?"

Al just simply looked at me and laughed that little laugh he had that indicated he was doing something that he should not be doing. "Are you going to get into trouble?" I asked.

About that time Steve whimpered, and I whispered, "Look, you've not seen your new son. Don't wake him up."

"Oh, Marilyn," he exclaimed. "He is beautiful."

"Handsome. He is handsome," I replied.

"No, he is beautiful," Al insisted. "He is a beautiful baby boy."

And he was. Most babies are beautiful, but honestly, Steve was exceptionally so. Al reached down and gently picked him up out of the bassinet and held him for most of the night. Steve obviously loved it because he snuggled up into his proud father's chest and slept, without waking, until dawn.

As the baby slept, Al told me the story of his adventure to arrive at my window in the middle of the night. He began, "When my sergeant told me you had given birth, I knew I had to come. I could not miss this exciting moment. So I talked to one of my buddies who agreed to answer for me at roll call this morning. As soon as we finished training yesterday, I left."

"Did you have permission?" I interrupted.

"No."

"No?" I snapped. "Can't you get into trouble for that?"

He replied very calmly. "Well, if I get caught, I'm AWOL and will probably spend some time in the stockade (which is army for jail). But I don't care! I had to be here. I knew it was almost 400 miles from Ft. Riley to Ft. Sill, so I had to hurry."

Continuing with his story, he said, "I put on a new uniform, left Ft. Riley, and started hitchhiking to Ft. Sill. I was blessed, because within a few minutes, a man driving to Chickasha, Oklahoma, stopped and gave me a ride. From there it was easy to find rides going to Ft. Sill. And, here I am!"

I asked him how he got to the hospital, and how did he possibly know what window to knock on in this very large hospital?

He said, "I snuck into Ft. Sill, avoiding military police, asked some guys about the location of the hospital and followed their directions. When I found the hospital, I simply walked in the front door and asked about your room. They told me what room you were in, but informed me in no uncertain terms that visiting hours were over and you and the baby were not to be disturbed. Since I had your room number, I looked at the room chart in the lobby and figured out which window was yours. I had already noticed the large fire escapes on the outside of the building. From there it was easy. I crawled up to the fire escape and made my way to your room. Thank God, you were willing to unlock the lock," he said with that wonderfully mischievous smile.

"Thank God, you are here," I replied and hugged him as he held our new son.

Al spent the rest of the night in my room, holding our baby.

Early the next morning, the doctors made their rounds. My doctor, the army colonel, walked in the room and was surprised to see Al. "Hey, solider," he said, "you got to come see your little family. Did they give you a weekend pass?"

"No sir, I just came without a pass," Al replied.

"You're here without a pass?" the colonel asked.

"Yes sir," Al said, "I had to be here today."

"I understand son," the doctor said, "but you do know you are AWOL?"

"Yes sir, I know," Al said firmly.

"Well, as far as I'm concerned, I never saw you and you never saw me," the doctor insisted. "And since I am probably the only military person you will see in this room today, I suggest you stay here as long as you desire, but try to leave in time to be back at Ft. Riley early in the morning."

"Yes sir," Al said saluting. "Thank you, sir."

The next day my parents drove Al to catch the train back to Ft. Riley. He returned to his unit, and those in charge never knew he was gone, or at least never said they knew.

Al Gets Transferred to Germany

When I was dismissed from the hospital, I returned to live with my parents until Al completed his basic training. Young army wives grow up quickly. In less than a year, I had gone from being a carefree teenager—the only daughter of a large farm family in Oklahoma, studying hard to graduate at the top of my senior class and working each night as a waitress in the 277 Diner in my small town—to the wife of a soldier away on duty and the mother of a newborn son. Even being with my parents, as wonderful and caring as they were, I felt alone because Al was gone.

When Al completed his basic training, we were hoping he might be assigned to Ft. Sill, or at least stateside, but that did not happen. Rather, his orders were for Schweinfurt, Germany. I was devastated! When he told me, I sat down and cried for hours. We had been apart for his entire basic training, and now he would be stationed overseas for at least another year. Al would miss the entire first year of our baby's life!

Catching a Flight to Germany with Steve and Darlene

We spent as much time together as we could before he departed for Germany. As we talked and prayed through our coming year apart, I felt the Lord leading me to enter college and at least accomplish something positive while Al was away. It was the right decision. While at school, I made friends with another student, Darlene Goss, who was also the wife of a soldier. To our surprise, her husband and Al were in the same battalion and knew each other.

One afternoon, Darlene told me she was leaving school to move to Germany and be with her husband. She encouraged me to do the same. Once I received all the details from her, I called

Al and told him about Darlene coming to Germany. He said, "You should come too!"

It seemed like a big undertaking, and so expensive. "How could we afford it?" I asked.

"Sell the car," Al insisted. "That would give us enough money for you to come. It will be wonderful!"

I agreed. "I will," I responded, "as quickly as I can."

Darlene was leaving in November and wanted me to go with her at that time. "My parents are making all the travel plans for me. I'll ask them to make the same arrangements for you," she insisted.

I was thrilled. I had never been out of the U.S., but now I was going to Germany to be with my husband and live with the German people for a full year.

My parents drove me to the airport in Oklahoma City to meet Darlene, and we were off to New York City. In those days, flying was an event, and people dressed up to fly. I dressed in a black suit with a black and white tweed hat, high heels and hose, a matching purse, and a large matching coat. In addition, of course, I carried my baby Steve and a large diaper bag. There were no Pampers in those days!

Because of our flight connections, we were required to spend the night in New York City. Darlene's parents had made reservations for us at a wonderful hotel in the middle of Manhattan. We were surrounded by the noise and excitement of the city that never sleeps. Darlene was determined that we must go see a

Broadway play. That was the last thing I wanted to do. I was so tired! "I can't go to a play, I have a baby with me," I exclaimed.

"Of course you can," Darlene demanded. "We'll dress little Steve up in a tux and he will fit right in." Darlene was very entertaining. So, baby and diaper bag in tow, Darlene and I spent the afternoon standing in line to get tickets for "Guys and Dolls" on Broadway. There we were, two teenage girls and an infant boy, on our own in New York City. People were very nice to us. One lady offered to help with Steve, but I was not about to let go of him, even for a moment. We got our tickets with time to spare before the play, found a small restaurant and shared hamburgers before heading back to the theater. Steve was wonderful. No tears, just eating, needing changes and sleeping. He could not have been better. We finally arrived back at the hotel and quickly went to sleep.

The next morning, we caught a taxi to the airport. We had never been in a taxi before, and didn't know the rules concerning fares. Our fare was $4.75 to the airport and Darlene gave the driver a $5 bill. When we got out of the cab, the driver started cursing and screaming. He kept yelling, "Come back, come back!"

Darlene walked back to the taxi and when she did, the driver threw a quarter at her, screaming all the while. Darlene and I just looked at each other and said, "Who knew?"

Challenges and Adventures in Germany

Finally, we were on our way to Germany. I had never been on a plane before and this was going to be a long, long trip. I did a lot of praying on that flight, not only for our safety, but also that Al had received all our instructions on arrival time, etc. I had no way of knowing what to expect. The trip was long, but the plane was wonderful. Our first stop was Newfoundland, then across the ocean to London, and finally into Frankfurt, Germany.

Deplaning was an adventure of its own. Darlene was loaded down with her own bags, which meant I had to manage my own. So, in my beautiful black suit I had worn just for Al, my little hat, high heels, my matching purse and coat, I walked down the stairs of the plane holding Steve, his blankets, my purse and my large diaper bag. I looked as though I had brought everything I owned, and practically did!

Just as he had promised, Al was there to meet the plane. As soon as I entered the terminal, I saw him. He came running to me, arms wide open and grabbed me, the bags and Steve in one huge hug. He kept kissing me and our baby, our baby and me, and then me and our baby. It was wonderful! Our little family was together, and would not leave each other again for twenty-seven years!

As soon as Al turned loose of Steve and me, he introduced Darlene and me to his friend, Sergeant Rogers, who had driven his car to pick us up. Darlene's husband was not able to leave the base and meet her, but Al assured her he was waiting to see her as soon as we arrived back at Schweinfurt. We gathered the bags from the plane, loaded the car, and were off to become residents of Schweinfurt, Germany.

The trip from Frankfurt to Schweinfurt was 100 miles of Bavarian beauty. Wonderful mountains and quaint villages were at every turn. Al was in heaven. Holding his infant son on his chest, he never took his eyes off of me. I could tell by looking in his face how much he loved me, and it was a wonderful feeling!

The closer we came to Schweinfurt, the more devastation from the war we saw. Schweinfurt was an industrial city of some 52,000 people located on the Main River in northern Bavaria, and served as a major center of wartime industry for the Nazis in World War II. As a result, the city was a major target of bombing during the war. Nearly 8,000 tons of bombs were dropped on Schweinfurt. The bombs left the city largely in ruins with half of the houses and 80 percent of the industrial buildings destroyed. Two thousand civilians were killed in the war. Much of Schweinfurt remained in ruins when we arrived. Since we lived in the city and not on the military base, it was like living in a war zone every day. But the people loved Americans, so we always felt wanted and safe.

Al leased a temporary apartment for us in the city. The apartment was two small rooms divided by a public hallway between each room. One served as our bedroom. It was very primitive with lots of windows and a tiny sink on the wall. The room across the hall was our kitchen. I had to lock the door to one of the rooms as I moved into the other. Later on, we were able to secure much nicer accommodations in a two-story, German family home. I was thrilled!

We made many new friends while living there. Amazingly, many of the German families became close friends. Living in a former war zone that had been so totally devastated was challenging for the German families and those of us stationed there with our soldiers.

We found a nice apartment with a German family in a small village just outside Schweinfurt. Herr and Frau Horlacher had a typically small German home with a small vegetable garden. They turned their upstairs into a small one-bedroom apartment. The only heat was a coal stove in a tiny kitchen. We placed Steve's crib in the kitchen as sometimes the weather was 40 below zero. We had no running water and used the faucet and hose in the garden for our water supply.

The Horlachers were very good people and attentive to us. Their three beautiful children, Monika, Helmut and Bruno were delights. Frau Horlacher's parents also lived with them. I was very intrigued by the way in which they managed to survive. Most of their luxuries were gone. For instance, Frau Horlacher did her laundry in a large, black kettle with a wood fire in the back yard. She stirred the towels, sheets and clothes with a long stick in the boiling water over the fire, and then lifted them with the stick to another massive kettle filled with cold water to rinse. It was difficult work, but work she was glad to have. She taught me to do my laundry the same way. My biceps became quite impressive!

The time in Germany was simultaneously challenging and exciting. Much of the time we were there, Al was away on maneuvers, which left me alone with our infant son. During that time, Frau Horlacher and I spent time together with our children inside the German culture and grew very close. We made daily excursions to the local bakery. I have never seen such beautiful bakery products. They were literally works of art. I never wanted to cut a cake and destroy the artwork. Bakeries were fun to visit and enjoy their products. However, the military told us to never eat the produce from the German economy. The Germans fertilized their gardens with human waste. Horse and wagons made daily trips to outdoor toilets picking up the waste. These wagons were called "honey wagons," and the waste was hosed onto vegetable gardens.

Red Markers

When Al was on leave and home, we became tourists. During one of our trips to see the beauty of the surrounding mountains and quaint villages, we almost got in serious trouble. Our friends, Sergeant Rogers and his wife, Jeanie, had their own car. Several weekends we drove with them to enjoy the mountains. We were all amazed that such remarkable beauty could be so close to the complete destruction of war. The sergeant drove us east of Schweinfurt one Saturday to visit the Bavarian mountains. The entire area was so beautiful. As we drove along, I began to notice a series of red markers around the trunks of the trees. The others were enjoying the views and seemingly did not notice the markers. Finally, I spoke up, "What are those red markers?"

"What markers?" Al asked.

"Have you not seen them?" I responded. "There, there's another one."

"Oh no," the sergeant said sharply. "We are in trouble. We've got to get out of here. We're in the Soviet area."

My heart began to pound! I was genuinely afraid! We were constantly warned by the military to never even set a foot on Soviet land!

One aspect of the German surrender in World War II was the division of Germany between the allied powers. That division produced two German nations: East and West. The boundary between the two nations ran just to the East of Schweinfurt, and we had inadvertently driven out of the West and into the East. Had we been caught, we would have been in real trouble, especially since our two husbands were American soldiers. In fact, we might never have been seen or heard from again! We knew the drill. Al and I began to pray that the Lord Jesus would keep us covered and hidden from view. All at once, we drove into the thickest fog. We could barely see, but we had a compass in the car. So we slowly followed the compass. Thankfully, the sergeant got us turned around and back into the West before we were stopped. Needless to say, we planned our outings much more carefully after that incident.

After a year filled with exciting new experiences and wonderful new friends, it was time to return home. Of course, we were thrilled, but leaving our friends was sad. We all promised we would stay in touch and not lose our friendship, but regrettably, we did not do so.

The army made our travel arrangements to return home and booked us on the Flying Tigers Airline. The plane was very nice. Since I was seven months pregnant with our second child and traveling with our baby boy, the airline placed us in the bulkhead seats and provided a canvas baby bed that hung on the wall in front of us which Steve promptly kicked down.

About an hour out of Frankfurt, the captain came on the intercom and said in a very calm reassuring voice, "Ladies and gentlemen, in about an hour we will be making an unexpected stop to check out a possible mechanical problem. Everything is fine, and there is no danger, but before we begin our flight across the Atlantic, we will take a short stop in Shannon, Ireland."

When we stopped, they took us into a small room where they gave us refreshments and assured us we would not be long. After a couple of hours, the airlines announced that the problem was more serious than expected, and that we will not be able to continue without a new plane which will not be available until tomorrow or later. They were providing lodging for us at a very nice local hotel and would do all they could to expedite our delay. Being seven months pregnant and struggling with an 18-month-old baby, my patience was sorely tested. I just wanted to get home!

The hotel was very nice. They encouraged us to take advantage of the time in Shannon, enjoy the restaurant and see the sights. Once we arrived in our room, I was exhausted and had to rest. Al decided to take Steve and see the city. I told him to go kiss the Blarney stone, not realizing the Blarney Castle was an hour and a half from Shannon. Had I known how dangerous it was to kiss the stone, I would never have mentioned it. Thankfully, Al refused my invitation.

We could not leave Shannon for three days, which provided an excellent time for me to rest and enjoy the hospitality of our wonderful Irish hotel. Finally, we boarded a new plane and departed for New York. After one night in New York, we landed in Oklahoma City, drove home to Cement and restarted our lives as civilians.

CHAPTER 7

CHASING OIL AND GROWING IN JESUS

After being grounded for three days in Shannon, Ireland, we were once again on board the plane with Flying Tigers Airlines heading to the good old USA! We landed in Oklahoma City right before Thanksgiving. Al received his honorable discharge from the army, and we left to rejoin the oil business and raise our little family in Oklahoma. Over the next 27 years, our lives would be spent chasing oil and gas, and growing in our relationship with the Lord Jesus.

One of my greatest personal joys was seeing my loving husband become a man of great faith. In the same way that Al was learning and succeeding in the oil field, he was growing in his knowledge, faith and confidence in the Lord Jesus and in the supernatural work of the Holy Spirit. Looking back over those years, there was a series of very special pastors and churches that came into our lives and challenged us to go deeper and deeper in our understanding and commitment to the Lord Jesus.

Our first home after the army was the small town of Cyril, Oklahoma. We found a darling, little white-framed house right on Highway 277, which was the main road running through the town. It was a perfect little house for us. The house had a nice covered front porch with a front door that opened into the living room. To the left of the living room were two small bedrooms and a bathroom. I was so pleased that part of the living room was a dining area divided by a beautiful archway where my black lacquer dining room set with rose decals fit perfectly. Beyond the dining area was my little kitchen. The house was not large, but it was just right for us, and allowed us to quickly settle into our new routine.

Al immediately returned to work for Tri-County Well Service Company and was once again working in the oil fields of southwest Oklahoma as the foreman of a workover rig. Since Cyril, Oklahoma was only five miles from my childhood home in Cement, this was a wonderful time for me. I reconnected with many of my high school friends who were now married and had children of their own, as well as my family and my precious grandmother.

Brynda Is Born

Not only was I expecting our second child in two months, my best friend and cousin, Carolyn was also pregnant. We were so excited when we discovered we were both due to give birth in January. Carolyn had found a wonderful doctor in Chickasha named Dr. Davis. She insisted I use her doctor, so I did. So here we were, two pregnant cousins named Marilyn and Carolyn, the daughters of twin sisters named Nettie and Hettie, and about to give birth just days apart. Her baby boy, Larry, arrived on January 16, and I quickly followed with my beautiful daughter, Brynda, on January 20, 1957.

Al's Injury

Unfortunately, Cyril was not all happy times. One afternoon, as I was enjoying my two sweet babies, I saw Bill Jackson, the husband of my Cousin Carolyn, running to my front door. Before he could knock, I opened the door, and said, "Bill, what are you doing here?"

"Marilyn," he muttered half out of breath, "Al has been hurt, and I've come to take you to the hospital in Chickasha."

"Hurt?" I demanded. "Is he going to be alright?"

"I'm not sure how badly he's hurt, but they want you to come quickly," Bill insisted.

My mind was running as fast as it could. At one moment, I was praying for my injured husband, at the next, I wondered out loud what I would do with my babies. Hearing my quandary as I talked to myself, Bill said calmly, "We'll take the children to your grandma's house. Your Aunt Nettie is expecting them and will take care of them for you."

Grandma lived right on the highway from Cyril to Chickasha. So I hurriedly packed two baby bags, grabbed the babies and was off to the hospital.

Al was seriously hurt. Growing up around oil and gas drilling in southwest Oklahoma, I had always been told that work on the drilling rigs was difficult and grueling. I was to repeatedly learn firsthand that work on a rig is also very dangerous.

When I arrived at the hospital, the doctors would not let me see Al in the emergency room. Instead, I was told he would soon be transferred to another room, and I was to wait for him there. The longer I waited, the more my fear and anxiety grew. Finally, the attending doctor came to the room and I was able to get the details I so desperately needed.

"Your husband has been badly hurt. His head was injured and he has lost a lot of blood. We have been able to repair the injury and replenish the blood. It will take a while, but I do think he will make a full recovery," the doctor stated very succinctly and professionally.

"What happened to him?" I asked as I began to cry, "Is he in great pain? Is he alert? Is he talking? Will there be permanent damage to his brain?"

"No, he is not in pain. We have him sedated right now," the doctor replied. "As soon as he awakens, we will bring him here to this room. I do not think he will have any permanent brain damage."

"What happened?" I asked again through my tears.

Seeing that I was in great fear and needed reassurance, the doctor sat down in a chair next to me and softly began, "I don't know all the details but I do know that he was struck in the head by a piece of equipment on the rig. He is lucky to have been wearing a steel helmet. It saved his life! The helmet was so severely crushed against his skull they had difficulty removing it from his head." He continued, "Since he lost a great deal of blood from the injury, I am concerned that he may have had some minor short-term brain damage. Because of that, I want to keep him in the hospital for a few days for observation. But I want to assure you, I do not believe he will have any lasting brain damage."

As the doctor was finishing, the orderlies opened the door and brought Al into the room on a hospital bed. Seeing him for the first time was a shock. Before we were married, Al told me of other major injuries he had experienced. But this time he was my husband and the father of my children, so the injuries were right before my eyes—not in the past. He was lying motionless before me on a hospital bed, heavily bandaged from his eyebrows up and over his entire head.

Throughout the night as I sat with Al, several of the men who had been with him when he was injured came to the hospital to check on him. Some of them took time to meet with me and explain the details of the accident on the rig. Al was working with some of the young inexperienced men who were known as "greenhorns," that is, they did not know the details of working on a drilling rig. As they explained, one of the most challenging tasks is mastering the placement of the actual pipe that is being used to drill the well.

As the pipe is taken from the pipe stand, to be inserted into the drill hole, one group of men work on the floor of the rig while a single man works on a small platform at the top of the rig, known as the Eagles Nest. Each drill pipe is around 30 feet long. As the well gets deeper, additional sections of pipe are connected at the top of the hole. The pipes screw together to make the drillstring as long as required for drilling. The whole length of pipe, or drillstring, is twisted by a rotating turntable that sits on the floor of the derrick. When the drill bit becomes worn or when a different type of drill bit is needed, the whole drillstring must be pulled out of the hole to change the bit. Each piece of pipe is unscrewed as they are removed from the drill hole and stacked nearby.

When the pipe is raised from the drill hole, one man on the rig floor pushes the end of the pipe to the side of the rig into an area known as the setback floor while the man at the top of the rig disconnects the pipe and lets the top of the pipe fall into what is called, the racking board. When the top of the pipe then falls over against the other pipe in the racking board, it does so with the entire weight and force of the 30-foot steel pipe.

The man working at the top of the rig did not see that Al was showing the young men how to place the pipe in the setback floor when he released the pipe to fall into the racking board against the other pipe. As a result, the pipe fell against Al, scissoring his head between the falling pipe and other pipe in the setback floor which crushed his steel safety helmet into his skull. The force of the pipe was so great it mashed his steel safety helmet into his head, making it difficult to remove the helmet. At the same time, the steel safety hat saved his life!

Just hearing the explanation of the accident from the men caused me to almost pass out. Even though I clearly understood what the doctor said, I was still frightened about the future. A single question haunted me. Would I ever truly have my husband back? As I sat throughout that long night, I kept returning to the reoccurring injuries that seemed to follow Al. My confidence that he would always be safe was shaken. But one positive word continually returned to my heart, "Thank God that tonight, my precious husband is alive!"

It was not a quick recovery, yet despite a bout with Bell's palsy, the doctors were right, and Al fully recovered from the accident on the rig. He returned to work, and I returned to caring for our little ones.

Brynda Was Healed!

We had barely gotten back to our normal routine when the owners of the house we were renting in Cyril decided to sell the house. So, while Al was getting back into his work schedule, I was looking for a new place for us to live. Since Cyril was only five miles from my hometown of Cement, I told Al that I wanted to find a place in Cement, if possible, so we could be closer to my family and they could spend more time with Steve and Brynda and help me with the babies when needed. He agreed. When I told my Grandma that I was looking for a place in Cement, she was excited!

"Oh, Marilyn, do you remember the Smith house right down from my house?"

"Yes," I said. "Is it available?"

"Yes," she nodded.

I was thrilled! The house was wonderful, and less than a quarter mile from Grandma on Highway 277. We quickly secured the house and made the move from Cyril. Al was busy every day with his job at Tri-County Oil, and I had my hands full with two babies under 3 years old. Like all mothers, having enough hands to keep them both safe, clothed, fed and happy was a never-ending challenge.

The only negative about our new home in Cement was a floor furnace placed right in the archway between the living room and dining room. I was constantly concerned that one of the children would be accidentally burned. On a cold, icy, January afternoon, I had the heat on trying to keep the house warm enough for my babies. The routine I had developed was to put both of them down for naps about the same time every afternoon. Steve was about 2 ½ years old and usually went to sleep first. That afternoon was no exception. Once he was asleep, I was able to place him in his bed with no problem. Brynda had just turned 1 year old and was learning to walk. She was so inquisitive about everything around her that it normally took a while to get her to sleep. But that afternoon, Brynda quickly fell asleep. I was thrilled. When I stood to take her to her bed, I noticed she needed a diaper change. So, not wanting to awaken her, I turned back to the couch where I had been sitting while getting her to sleep, placed her on the couch and removed the wet diaper. I opened the diaper basket I kept next to the couch, and it was empty. The fresh diapers were in my bedroom. I tucked the blanket securely around her, and thought she would be safe while I quickly grabbed a clean diaper. I was wrong!

As soon as I opened the drawer and reached in to get the new diaper, Brynda screamed at the top of her voice. I dropped the diaper and ran to get her. When I saw her, she was sitting on the furnace with her little bare bottom. I could literally smell her flesh burning. Somehow, she had gotten off the couch, and probably wanting to come to me, walked toward the bedroom. When she stepped on the furnace she burned her little feet, and not knowing what to do, she sat down on the furnace without her diaper.

I immediately picked her up and wrapped her in a blanket. Brynda continued to scream out in pain. Somehow I managed to reach into Steve's bed and pick him up out of his sleep. When I did, he woke up and with Brynda screaming and crying he began to cry. Holding both of them, I walked across our snow covered yard, opened the car door, placed both of them on the seat next to me and drove as fast as I could to Dr. Dixon's office. I lifted both of them from the car and made my way through the ice and snow and into the doctor's office with both of them screaming at the top of their little voices. They knew me well at Dr. Dixon's office, especially since he was the doctor who brought me into the world 21 years before.

"Is he in?" I shouted to his nurse as I crashed through the door.

"What's wrong Marilyn?" she asked.

"Brynda has been badly burned! Please hurry!" I begged. She quickly took me to the examination room where Dr. Dixon was waiting.

"Let me see her," he said compassionately.

"She sat on the floor furnace," I explained as I began to cry.

"I can tell," Dr. Dixon replied. "She'll be okay, Marilyn. You relax, everything will be fine."

The nurse took Steve from me and was caring for him as I focused in on Brynda. She was crying and screaming at the top of her voice, but Dr. Dixon was unfazed. I had known this wonderful doctor my entire life. Just being in his office assured me that he would know what to do and Brynda would be safe. Dr. Dixon took her and placed a little cloth with chloroform across her face, and in just a short moment she passed out. With her anesthetized, he placed medication on each of the burns, then wiped the medication off and repeated the process several times. When he completed applying the medication, he bandaged the burns. Then he turned to me for my instructions.

"Marilyn," Dr. Dixon directed, "she has been seriously burned. This will take a while to heal. She will be in real pain for at least two weeks, which means she will do a lot of crying. I want you to cut an aspirin into fourths, break it up and give it to her every four hours for the pain. These burns are deep and they will blister. Do not put her in water, and do not put water on the burns. Do you understand?"

"Yes, I understand," I whispered. "Will she be scarred?" I asked.

He thought for a minute, and answered, "She is so young, I doubt if she will be scarred, but if she is it will probably only be on her little bottom."

The nurse helped me place both of them back in my car, and we returned home. Brynda was groggy from the chloroform when we arrived, but within a few minutes after we got home, she began to cry. I gave her the aspirin, rocked her for nearly an hour and finally got her to sleep. As she slept, she whimpered softly, and I cried. I could not believe something so tragic could happen to my precious daughter, especially while I was with her.

When Al arrived home that evening, he had not been told of the accident, but could quickly tell I was upset, and saw that I had been crying. Instead of his usual greeting, he looked at me and asked, "What's wrong? Everything okay?"

Through my tears, I explained what had happened. When I told him, he simply walked back to Brynda's room, got down on his knees, laid his head over on her bed and started to pray for about twenty minutes. Then he stood, looked back at me, and whispered, "She's healed!"

My doubts were strong because the burns were deep. I tried to smile, and when I did, Al walked over and held me for several minutes, gave me his normal greeting kiss and walked in our bedroom to change clothes.

And indeed, Brynda was healed! She never cried again. And even though the burns were deep and turned red, there were no blisters, ever. The Lord Jesus had heard the prayer of her daddy and healed her little body!

CHAPTER 8

A MOVE TO FARMINGTON, NEW MEXICO

Oil and gas drilling in southwest Oklahoma finally slowed, and as it did, Al and I faced financial uncertainty for the first time in our marriage. We both knew that to keep pace with drilling activity, we would probably have to move away from Cement. As we were praying and seeking the leadership of the Lord for our little family, my Uncle Luke called Al and told him of the exciting oil and gas discoveries taking place in the Four Corners area around Farmington, New Mexico, and encouraged him to come to work there. The report of a boom in oil drilling taking place in Farmington was very exciting, and we immediately knew that this was the direction we must take.

We sold what we could to afford the move, loaded our car and a small trailer with our few essential belongings and made the move to Farmington. When we arrived, Uncle Luke provided the money for us to rent a place to live in a very nice mobile home park. Unfortunately, Uncle Luke was not able to hire Al to work on his drilling rigs at that time, but he told Al to go to the City Cafe in downtown Farmington and post a short one-page resume on the bulletin board.

"Al, I promise you someone will hire you immediately."

Al followed his direction and posted his availability on the board. Since we had no phone, Al simply left our address. Sure enough, bright and early the next morning, a man knocked on our door and offered Al a job. He graciously accepted it and went to work that day.

However, the problem was that we had no money! And I do mean, no money! Had it not been for my Uncle Luke, we wouldn't have had a place to live either. Thank God for the job Al got on our first day in Farmington, but I still needed money to feed my children before he received his first paycheck two to three weeks later.

We had faithfully tithed and given offerings to our churches since the very first day of our marriage, and as He always does, the Lord Jesus has always blessed us. Now, our backs were against the wall. As I prayed that morning, a knock came on the door.

"Mrs. Wheeler, I am the local milkman. I deliver to most of the homes here in the park. I have all the dairy products. In fact,

I have almost every essential except bread. If you want, I could set you up on an account, and you can pay me every 30 days."

I wanted to drop to my knees right there in front of the man and start thanking the Lord Jesus. I'm sure he could see the joy and thankfulness on my face. So, before I could say a word, he continued, "What do you need today?"

I blurted out, "Everything. I need everything!"

"Well," he said. "Let's get you everything."

I shook my head, and thankfully said, "Thank you, thank you so much."

When Al arrived home late that night from his first day at work, we both had good news to share. I took him in the kitchen and opened the refrigerator. It was filled with all the wonderful items I received from the milk man. I was so excited. As Al gave me a huge celebration hug, I said, "Honey, we have everything but bread."

"Well," he responded, "I've got the bread!"

His new company told him as he was leaving work that day that if he needed anything, we could come by the office and they would front us some money. We quickly got the children dressed and headed to the company office. Neither of us knew exactly what to expect, but anything would help. Al went in to meet with his employers and came back to the car with a $5 bill. He was smiling ear to ear. It was only $5—but it was enough for bread. In the 1950s, you could buy a lot with five dollars!

We rejoiced and thanked the Lord Jesus for His provision. Even though Al would not be paid for a couple of weeks, he had a good job, we had our little family, we had food and a wonderful place to live. We were blessed!

I'll Do It!

The very first thing we did was look for a new church home. It was an easy task. The first Sunday we attended the First Assembly of God in Farmington, we knew this was the place for us, and it was. The church would prove to be the center of our lives and the place of our greatest growth as a young Christian family. We quickly loved our pastor, Brother Melvin Sassey, and he quickly loved us. The church became our place of friendship, service and growth.

Al's job on the drilling rig was very demanding. He worked 12-hour shifts and in order to provide more for us, he often pulled double shifts. Since he was with a new company that did not know his talents, he had to start out once again on the floor of the rig. Soon, his abilities were obvious to those in management and promotions came quickly. He moved from laborer to driller to managing the rig. Of course, with more responsibilities came greater time demands, but he managed to succeed in his work, have time for me and the children, and become very involved with the church.

Pastor Sassey became a genuine friend to Al. In many ways, the two of them counted on one another. Al was so positive and affirming to Brother Sassey, and the pastor was a challenging mentor to Al. It was obvious to anyone that there was a special call of God on Al. His love for the Lord Jesus and his commitment to the work of the church was overwhelming. When Brother Sassey would say they needed someone to visit the jail, or pray for the sick in the hospital, or help with some task at the church, Al would immediately reply, "I'll do it!"

He was so gung-ho. I had grown up in the church and around the ministry and had seen the struggle pastors and churches have to get people to work in the church and support the ministry. But Al was unique. The work of the ministry became the center of his life, and thus the center of our lives. Each Sunday afternoon, we were doing the work of the church, and loving almost every minute of it. I could go with Al to the hospitals and pray for the sick. He prayed for everyone, even if they did not want to be prayed for. Someone would say, "Not me, you don't need to pray for me. I don't need anything."

Al always responded, "Well then, you really do need me to pray."

And he would. When he prayed, God always moved, and almost always, people would be healed. As soon as he prayed, the individuals were thrilled saying, "Thank you Al, thank you. I am so glad you prayed for me." It was truly amazing!

The only place I was hesitant to go with him was to the jail. I may be showing my lack of faith, but when those doors would clang shut and the guards would turn the locks, I became so claustrophobic that I simply could not take it! I told Al, "I will go to the hospitals, but not the jails."

He would laugh and say, "Of course you can go to the jails. The women love you." He would assure me and love me right through my fears, and of course, I went to the jails.

Our House in Farmington

The Lord Jesus blessed us in Farmington. With Al's increasing responsibilities in the oil field, he began to make very good money, so much so, that we were able to purchase a brand-new home and even a brand-new car. Life was good. Our new home—did I mention it was a brand new home?—was the first home we had actually owned.

The house was a typical southwest New Mexico style. It was stucco with a flat roof and large wooden poles protruding out from around the top of the house and turquoise accents. There were three bedrooms, a wonderful living room and a kitchen with adequate space for a table and chairs. The floors were all tile. When they were waxed, they were so beautiful.

Al built a redwood fence around our large backyard for our little ones. We planted grass, flowers and trees and in no time with the warm New Mexico weather our yard looked great. Inside the single car garage of our brand new home was a brand new blue and white two-tone Mercury. We were thrilled and so proud of our new house and car.

Al Received the Baptism of the Holy Spirit

One Sunday evening, many people went to the altar to pray about various matters. Al joined them. As the evening progressed, most of the people had left the service. Only a handful remained, including Al, who was kneeling at the prayer altar. Brother Sassey was sitting on the platform and spoke to Al, "Al, come up here, I want to pray for you to be baptized in the Holy Spirit."

Al obeyed, and joined the pastor on the platform. The pastor laid his hands on Al's head and prayed for the Lord Jesus to baptize him with the Holy Spirit. When the pastor prayed over him, Al stepped back and fell off the platform and over the prayer altar, and came up speaking in tongues! I could only hope he hadn't broken his neck or something! When he realized he wasn't injured, we got a good laugh out of his misstep. But, it was an incredible experience that further heightened Al's commitment to the Lord Jesus and His church.

Once Al received the baptism of the Holy Spirit, he began to receive opportunities to speak at various churches and events around the Four Corners area. The more the Lord used Al and blessed his work in the ministry, the more Al began to believe the Lord was calling him into the full-time ministry. He said to me one day, "You know Marilyn, if the Lord is calling us into the ministry, you're going to need to learn to play the piano, and I'm going to need to play the guitar."

At first, I thought he was joking. He wasn't!

Early one morning as I was feeding the children, a moving truck pulled up in front of our house, and men unloaded a large crate. One of the men walked up on the porch. When he did, I met him at the door.

"Mrs. Wheeler?" he asked.

"Yes," I replied.

"We have your new piano for you," he said with a pleasant smile.

"A piano?" I said in shock.

"Yes, your husband said to get it right out to you as soon as possible. Where do you want it?"

I turned from the door to survey the room and decided it would probably fit best against the wall in the living room against the kitchen. When they finished placing the piano against the wall, the man handed me a stack of books and said, "Your husband also purchased these books for the beginning pianist. He said you were very committed to learning to play."

After they left, I stood looking at the piano almost in a trance until one of the children cried out from neglect in the kitchen. I mumbled to myself, "Just wait until he gets home."

Al walked in the door late that evening and did not give me a chance to speak before he blurted out, "Did you get it?" I knew he had already seen the piano sitting in the living room. It could not be missed.

"Get what?" I asked sarcastically.

"The piano," he responded, "don't you love it? You will be so good at playing the piano. I just know it! You're going to love it!"

I could not tell if he were trying to convince me or himself. I tried to assure him I could never learn to play, but he was certain this was the will of God, and the Holy Spirit would help me learn quickly! As he went on and on about me learning to play the piano, I interrupted him and asked tersely, "Well, where's your guitar?"

To my surprise, he said, "It's in the car. I'll get it out right now."

Off he went to the car, and brought back in a new Fender guitar, the best money could buy. "Honey," he announced, "Fender is the very best guitar. And since we are doing this for Jesus, we need to have the very best!"

I knew my complaints were useless, and simply said, "That's wonderful."

Every day when Al would come home, he would ask me about the piano and if I were practicing and learning to play church hymns. I assured him I had. I really had read the books, and tried to work on some of the fundamentals, but I was a long way from being able to play the piano. I had no idea how quickly I would be put to the test.

The Navajo reservation dominated northwest New Mexico. The reservation was dotted with small towns, and there were Indian churches in each of those towns. Once Al began speaking, several of those churches asked him to come and preach. The

Indian people responded well to Al and the stories he weaved throughout his sermons. One Sunday morning we drove to the tiny town of Kirtland where the pastor of the Indian church, who was going to be absent, had invited Al to preach.

When it was time for the service to begin, it was learned that the piano player and the worship leader could not come that Sunday. Al knew exactly what to do. He stood up and told the congregation, "Don't worry. My wife, Marilyn, plays the piano. She can play for the service, and I'll lead the worship."

I shrank down in my seat, gave him the most piercingly negative look I could, and pleaded, "Not me. I'm not ready to play. I have a baby to hold."

A woman offered to hold my baby girl. So, there I stood empty handed and with no excuse. Al just continued, "Come on, Marilyn, don't be bashful; come on, you can do it. Come on."

With no way out that I could see, I slowly made my way to the little piano and took my place. Al stood and began to lead the one song he thought I knew, "No, Not One." I had no idea what I was doing. I knew you were supposed to push the metal peddle at the bottom of the piano up and down with your foot. So, I got my foot in place. Once Al started singing, I just tried to follow along. As the song went up, I went up on the keyboard, and as the song went down, I went down on the keyboard. I was so furious. All I could think was, "Al Wheeler, you have had it when we get home."

Finally, the song service mercifully ended. I stood from the piano to walk back to my seat. When I did, the people were so precious, they actually applauded, and I was ready to faint. When the service was over, many came up to me and told me how much they enjoyed my piano playing. I was shocked. The only explanation I can give is that God gave me a miracle in that moment and enabled me to play well enough to help the people worship. I have never played the piano again!

The Angel Is Right Around the Next Curve

Supernatural manifestations became more and more common in our lives as Al grew in his remarkable faith and confidence in the Lord Jesus and the work of the Holy Spirit. As we left for an unavoidable road trip one cold, snowy, icy night which would take us through the mountains between Farmington and Albuquerque, I told of my concern about the bad driving conditions. Al turned to me in the car and said, "Don't worry, tonight as we are driving in the mountains, there will be several curves, and one of them is severe and very dangerous. I want you to know that on that curve there will be a large angel who will be there to protect us. I don't want you to worry or be afraid when you see him."

I stared at Al for just a moment, and muttered, "How do you know that?"

"I just know. The Holy Spirit just told me," he answered. And with that he started the car and we departed for Albuquerque. Later that night as we were making our way through the mountains, I was talking to Al, when he interrupted me, and said softly, "The angel is right around this next curve."

And he was right. The curve was extremely sharp and snow-packed, but as we reached the worse point, we saw him. On the right side of our car, standing between us and the canyon drop off was a magnificent angel, clothed in white, standing with his arms folded as a sentinel who had to be at least 10 feet tall. Al kept slowly driving, but I stared at him, transfixed and turned to see him through the side windows and out the back. As we safely made our way around the curve, the angel slowly disappeared. I watched out the back window for some time hoping the angel would again appear, but he did not. Then I turned back to Al and could not stop talking, "That was unbelievable! That was amazing! Did you see that? Did you see how tall he was? Did you see his eyes? I've got chill bumps all over me! I've never seen anything like that in my life," and on and on. Finally, I caught my breath, and asked Al, "Does this happen to you a lot?"

"Sometimes," he replied, and we drove on through the night.

The work of the Lord Jesus and His church grew more and more important and exciting to Al. He was constantly accepting new opportunities for us to minister. Al genuinely felt God was calling us into full-time ministry. He even decided to enter Southwestern Assembly of God College in Waxahachie, Texas and prepare for the ministry. Since we believed he could go to school on the GI Bill, he applied right away. But to our deep disappointment, we were informed the GI Bill had lapsed by about a month. We felt that door had closed, but that would not keep us from being involved in the ministry of the Lord Jesus. From that time forward, Al determined in his heart to go to the top in the oil business and serve the church in any way possible.

Right after the disappointment concerning Al's decision to enter the ministry, he was seriously hurt once again. Working late into the night on a rig, Al was struck by a pipe, knocked off the drilling rig and broke both the clavicle bone in his shoulder and the humerus bone at the top of his arm. Once again, a serious injury hospitalized my husband. The injuries seemed to be constant. Year after year, he was seriously hurt. But as always, he healed quickly and headed right back to work and right back to speaking at every opportunity.

Despite the injuries, our years at Farmington were very good for us. Al and I both grew personally, professionally, financially and most of all spiritually. We developed wonderful friends and began in earnest our life of commitment to the work of the church.

THE TARGET

CHAPTER 9

A MOVE BACK TO OKLAHOMA

After about five years in Farmington, despite wonderful friends we developed while there, we were anxious to get back to Oklahoma. Al and I were both praying for a great opportunity to open for us to return home. Our children were growing, and it was important to us that they have a relationship with their grandparents and other relatives.

Early one morning, Al received a call that changed our lives for the next seven years. Fred Jones was a renowned Ford car dealer in Oklahoma, yet few people knew that he was also a major investor and operator in the oil field. The woman on the phone greeted Al and said, "Mr. Wheeler, Fred Jones would like to speak with you. Are you available?"

"Yes, I am," Al responded. "But can you tell me what this is about?"

"I believe he wants to speak with you about employment with Hall-Jones Oil Company," the woman answered.

Al assured her he would be willing to meet with Mr. Jones and his oil people, which he did. They wanted Al to become the production manager of the oil and gas wells owned by Hall-Jones. It was a great offer with an increase in pay. We were both thrilled, so Al began a decade-long relationship with Hall-Jones Petroleum.

The new position of production manager for oil and gas wells owned by Hall-Jones was a dream opportunity for Al. It placed him at the forefront of the oil and gas industry in Oklahoma and dramatically changed our lives. God blessed Al and opened his talent to leading independent oil and gas companies. His work was recognized and appreciated.

They made him a terrific offer: to oversee their working wells around the Oklahoma City area. The most wonderful aspect of this offer for me was that Al would not be working directly on the drilling rigs every day, all day long. He had worked on the drilling platforms since he was a teenager and been hurt several times, so the thought of him being in a safer position was greatly welcomed.

The opportunity to be back in Oklahoma was an answer to our prayers. To make the opportunity even better, we would live in Oklahoma City! Growing up in Oklahoma, Oklahoma City was the place to be and the thought of living in the "big city" with all the opportunities, was very exciting. As we prayed about the decision, both of us knew that this job offer was a blessing from God and quickly accepted the new position.

We sold our home in Farmington, packed up our things, and made the move to our new home on Northwest 34th Street in Oklahoma City. The house was two stories with a large finished attic. It was really very nice. Both of us loved being there, and Al loved his new position as well. Managing a large number of active wells meant he was busy each day, but since the work was usually within driving distance to Oklahoma City, he was home almost every night and weekends.

Daddy, Help Me!

One of the very special features of our new home was a large oak tree in the backyard. It was the perfect tree for a treehouse, so Al built a very special one for our 6-year-old son, Steve. Steve loved the treehouse, and practically lived in it. The treehouse was filled with everything a little boy could want, especially a rope, which he used as a way to descend back to the ground. Although the treehouse was only about 6 feet off the ground, I warned him over and over to be careful, and usually he was, but early one morning as he played, he climbed on top of the treehouse and continued climbing about 20 feet up in the tree.

Al was watching him from the window, when suddenly Steve lost his grip and fell straight to the ground landing on his stomach and face. Al immediately ran to him. He bent over and turned Steve over on his back. As he did, Steve was gasping for breath. He looked up to his dad and said, "Daddy, help me!"

Steve's little face was white as snow. He kept trying to fall to sleep and Al kept shaking him to keep him awake. Al said later that both of his legs and arms appeared to be broken, and one leg was twisted backwards. I was trying to call for an ambulance, but my hands were shaking so badly I could not even dial the phone. In the meantime, Al was praying over Steve.

Al worked with one of the medic groups in the army and had learned to recognize the danger signs after a fall. He had seen his little brother killed by a fall from a horse, and a second brother accidentally shot and killed while playing "guns" with a little friend. These tragedies were running through his mind as he examined Steve. Al was taking no chances with his own son. He continued his prayers over Steve.

"Does your head hurt?" Al asked. "Does your stomach hurt?" Al continued with his examination. Finally, he believed Steve could move. He reached down, picked him up and brought him into the house and placed him on the couch. I ran over, washed his face with a cold cloth and held him for a moment as Al continued to pray for him. He told Steve not to move his legs, and then his arms. Steve seemed to be stabilized. As color returned to Steve's face, Al believed God had done a miracle in Steve's body. When Al returned to the living room, he picked Steve up, turned to me and said, "Steve is going to work with me."

"He's been hurt," I insisted.

"He'll be fine with me," Al replied.

Al made a bed for him in the backseat of his car, and Steve spent the day with his dad, and Al spent the day praying for his son. When they returned home that evening, Steve was his usual self, full of energy and ready to head for his treehouse, but his Dad said no. The treehouse was empty for the next several days.

I was so thrilled to see my precious little boy perfectly well, and to see the faith and confidence in his father. There were never any repercussions from Steve's fall. Whatever was hurt when he fell was healed when he spent the day with his dad.

Al Prayed and People Were Healed

One of the first decisions we had made when we moved was to find a really good church. In our search, the Holy Spirit led us to a wonderful Assembly of God church pastored by Brother Harold Powell. He was a powerful pastor who became a great friend to Al and me. Our faith grew under his leadership, especially Al's love and commitment to the healing power of the Lord Jesus. I will always believe that our time with Pastor Powell prepared Al to pray healing for our little boy and also launched Al into a new level of faith for healing. From that point forward, Al loved to pray for individuals who were sick or injured, and most of those for whom he prayed were immediately healed. It was obvious that Al's ministry was in divine healing. He just happened to be close when people were sick or hurt, and he prayed them well.

Regrettably, our time in Oklahoma City was limited. Once Hall-Jones saw the talent Al had to operate and manage their interest in Oklahoma, he quickly became the one they turned to when a field needed to be turned around and made more productive. One of those fields was around Hill City, Kansas. We were moving again!

CHAPTER 10

HILL CITY, KANSAS

I was so excited about living in a large, thriving city like Oklahoma City and wanted my children to have the opportunities that came from living in a large city. Hill City, Kansas was the exact opposite. Where Oklahoma City was the state capital surrounded by a million people, Hill City was a small town in a county of less than 5000. But like Oklahoma City, Hill City was absolutely surrounded by major oil and gas production. In fact, the area around Hill City was the location of one of the major oil and gas discoveries in the U.S. Once we arrived, it was obvious why Hall-Jones wanted Al to be there.

We leased a large stone house a few miles from the town and settled into our routine. Al's job was demanding. He was managing 40 to 50 producing wells, which meant every day he checked the wells to insure they were working properly, and called in help for those that required it.

Steve and Brynda were in grade school, making new friends and enjoying our new country house. I was busy putting together a new home and caring for each of my little ones which meant I was busy around the clock. We were also all enjoying our new baby girl, Sandi, who was born in 1963.

Our very first Sunday in Hill City, as was our custom, we found a church to attend. Since we loved First Assembly of God in Farmington, we found First Assembly in Hill City. It was wonderful! Brother Dan McGraw, a young man with remarkable wisdom and love for the Lord Jesus, was the pastor. He and his precious wife, Joan, quickly became our close friends. Al was older than the pastor, and as a result, was able to be a great resource to him. Simultaneously, Pastor McGraw constantly challenged Al in his walk with the Lord Jesus. Al and I both grew spiritually while we were there and were deeply thankful for his ministry and the church.

As usual, the church was the center of our lives. We were faithful in our attendance, with our service, in our giving and our commitment to the overall life of the church. Just as we had experienced in Farmington, our friends came from the church, and they were wonderful. There was a group of young couples who were our age. As would be expected, we were drawn to them, and they to us. These relationships made our time in Hill City very special.

Jerry Was Healed!

Al's faith and confidence in the healing power of the Lord Jesus continued to grow. He had reached the place where his prayers for healing were immediately answered. Again and again, situations would happen which put him right at the place where a miracle was necessary. One such instance occurred on a moonless night at the drilling rig. Al was not usually at the rigs late, but something had gone wrong and he was there to work it through with the drilling crew. A young "greenhorn" named Jerry was assisting on the rig when a pipe broke loose and was swinging freely on the rig. Rather than getting out of the way of the pipe, Jerry reached to grab it. When he did, the pipe knocked him off the floor of the rig some 25 feet to the ground where he landed on some stacked pipe.

As soon as he hit the ground, Jerry started screaming out in pain for help. The crew immediately gathered around him and was about to lift him up when Al shouted out, "Don't move him!" and ran to his side.

It was obvious to Al that Jerry had broken his back. He turned to the men crowded around and asked them to get on the radio and call an ambulance. Then Al began to pray. He laid his hands on him and prayed for about ten minutes. When he stopped, he looked at Jerry and said, "How are you feeling?"

"Better," Jerry replied.

Al told him to hold still and not move. "I'll stay right here with you until the help gets here."

When the ambulance arrived, Al was confident of Jerry's healing, but insisted he go in the ambulance to the hospital ASAP. At the end of the day, Al called the hospital for a report on Jerry. The report was not good! Jerry had broken his back in four places. The surgery had been long and Jerry was still in the recovery room.

That evening, Al and I visited him after Jerry was returned to his room. The antiseptic had worn off and he was suffering. We prayed for Jerry and for a peaceful and restful night. Jerry stayed in the hospital for a week, but then asked his wife to drive him to the drilling rig. When they arrived, Al went to his car and visited with both of them. Jerry maintained that he had been healed and wanted to return to work on the rig. Al told him he could not return to work until his cast was removed and he was released by the doctors.

Jerry then proceeded to get out of the car and struggled to walk up and down the stairs of the rig platform. He told Al, "I am healed! I know I am. I just need to get out of this cast!" In his unwavering faith, Al also believed he was healed. So, Al got a power saw and cut the body cast off Jerry! Once Jerry was free of the body cast, he ran circles around the rig and went back to work immediately!

Jerry grabbed a 100-pound bag of cement and carried it up 10-12 stairs to the rig floor. Then he went back down and repeated the process until he had 30-40 bags of dry cement on the rig floor. Jerry was back at work and never had another back pain or problem. Jerry's miracle of healing was a great testimony to the men on the rig. As a result, several of them accepted Jesus as Lord and Savior and became devout Christians.

Sadly, not all our time was as delightful. Two of the families in our church experienced tragedies that shook our church and our lives. The Ganos were a major family in First Assembly. They had been instrumental in starting the church and used their wealth to underwrite the work of the church, especially in its opening years. One afternoon, Gayln Gano was killed in a head-on collision just a few miles from Hill City. The church was stunned and quickly rallied to minister to the family. I will never forget going to the Gano home that evening to share our concern and express our sympathy. Gayln's wife, Jean, was in her bedroom lying on her back with her head falling off the bed. I wondered for a moment if she were dead. I leaned over and asked softly, "Jean, are you OK?"

Without raising her head, she weepingly said, "I'll never be OK!"

That moment overwhelmed me. My own husband had been hurt again and again, hospitalized repeatedly for various accidents and barely escaped being killed in a major car wreck. If he were to die, would I ever be OK again? I had always felt secure about Al. Regardless of the injuries he experienced, we were Christians, and Christians were supposed to be safe. Yet, the Ganos' were great Christians, and he was tragically killed! That was very confusing to me. I remember clearly thinking, how could a great Christian man so easily be killed? Where was the Lord? I began to wonder if God could be entrusted with our lives.

Allen Riggs was the postmaster in Hill City. He and his family were committed members of our church, including their beautiful daughter, Becky. She was a few years older than our children and had helped us out as a babysitter several times. Then tragedy struck! On a beautiful summer morning, Becky drowned in a local motel pool. The shock of her death was devastating, especially in our church, and for me. It raised so many questions. How could my family be safe if two major families were struck down by death so early in their lives? I began to question, "Where was God?"

Pastor McGraw preached both funerals. I felt for him. What could he possibly say that would explain the heartbreaking deaths of these two wonderful Christians? He admitted in his sermon that the only thing he could do was admit that we will never understand how something like this could happen, but we could be assured that they were with the Lord Jesus in heaven. It was a very sad time!

Life went on. But I could not shake off the uneasiness I felt over these two tragedies. It seems they both had a large target on their backs. Where was our divine protection? I began to question God over and over. I knew the Bible says there is a time to be born and a time to die. I knew we would all die, but I had been taught that God promises Christians will live 70 years. And little Becky was only 11 years old!

You Would Be Perfect for the Job

The home we leased in Hill City was owned by a doctor who practiced at the local hospital and who soon became our family physician. On one of my visits to him with the children, he told me that the hospital was looking for a person to help with the front office and the admission of new patients, and encouraged me to apply for the position.

"Marilyn," he said confidently, "you would be perfect for this job. You are so good with people. You would be a natural."

"Thank you, but there is no way I could do that," I responded.

I was certain that Al would not want me to work and be away from the house when he was home; and besides, I was way too busy with my three children and my work with the church. But for some reason, I could not quit thinking about the possibility of working at the hospital.

About a week later, I brought the subject up with Al, and to my surprise, he was open to the idea. We talked about the hours I would work, what we would do with the children and a score of other aspects of taking the position. He was absolutely supportive, and I was genuinely thrilled. After we finished talking, Al looked at me and said, "If this is something you want to do, then I think you should do it. It can't hurt to apply. Fill out the application, and let's see. If they offer you the job, we'll work it out."

So, with my husband's support, I went to the hospital and submitted my application. As soon as I completed the forms, they told me I had the job. I was thrilled. Once they told me my salary, I was doubly thrilled. As soon as Al arrived home that evening, I told him. He was surprised, but delighted.

"You mean they have already offered you the job?" he asked.

"Yes, it's my position if I want it. I would work from 3:00 until 11:00 p.m. Monday through Thursday."

Al was excited with me and proud of me. He responded, "Well, you've got to do it. It will be good for you and for us." As we talked, we agreed that I would be home with baby Sandi during the day, and he would pick Steve and Brynda up from school. Then he would come home and be with the children in time for me to be at work by 4:00 p.m.

I loved having the job. I started by registering new patients, and it was very enjoyable. During my first year, I learned that many people and insurance companies owed the hospital a large amount of money and had not paid. So when I was not busy registering new patients, I began calling those individuals and companies and worked out payment plans for them. As a result, I was bringing in thousands of dollars to the hospital each week. The administrator and directors were thrilled, and quickly moved me into a management position as assistant administrator of the hospital. About a year later, the administrator of the hospital had me come to his office and told me he and the board wanted to train me over the next year to take his position. He was retiring, and the board was so pleased with my work and wanted me to become the administrator of the hospital. They sent me to college in Ft. Hayes, Kansas where I was training for this position. I was thrilled!

My success at the hospital was very good for me. I had married very young and was always dependent on my husband to take care of our children and me, and he did provide for us, wonderfully. But the hospital position gave me a renewed confidence in my ability and assured me that I was gifted and capable. That capability would serve me well for the rest of my life. When I learned that Al's company was transferring us back to Oklahoma before I could finish my training and take the position as administrator, I was sad, but I was excited to go back home to Oklahoma.

THE TARGET

CHAPTER ELEVEN

THE RETURN TO OKLAHOMA

Hall-Jones Oil and Gas was a major player in the oil and gas fields around Enid, Oklahoma, and needed Al's expertise to bring the wells up to their full potential. What he had accomplished in Hill City, the company wanted him to do with their wells in northwest Oklahoma.

By now, our routine was established. We found a nice home to lease in a good neighborhood with good schools for our children; the first Sunday in Enid, we found the First Assembly of God church, and we were set. The church was great! It was the largest church we had ever attended as a family and as with most large churches, their ministries for our children were outstanding.

Al Injured Again

One afternoon as I was unpacking, I ran across an ad for hospitalization insurance that would pay $100 a day directly to the injured party for every day they were in the hospital. This was in addition to the hospitalization we had through Al's company. I had seen ads like this before, but for some reason I felt drawn to this offer, and immediately applied and was accepted.

About a month later, we needed the insurance. Al was making his rounds, checking the Hall-Jones wells for which he was responsible. At one rig location, he noticed that the amount of drilling pipe was getting low so he began to count the pipe to see the number of stands that remained. But to do so, he had to climb up on the pipe which was stacked on metal stands. As he was bent over counting the pipe in one stand, the pipe on which he was standing broke loose and sent Al and the pipe tumbling to the ground. When he hit the ground, the pipe hit him.

Steve and Brynda had just arrived home from school when a man I recognized from Hall-Jones Petroleum came to the door. I immediately knew that Al was hurt. As soon as I opened the door, I asked, "Is he badly hurt?"

"Yes, Mrs. Wheeler," he replied. "He's very badly hurt. They have taken him to the Enid hospital, and they want you to come immediately."

"Let me call and get help with my children, and I'll be ready," I replied.

I called a friend from our new church, and they were at our home in just a few minutes. On the way to the hospital, I realized I was not filled with fear or dread. Al and I had been together for nearly ten years while he worked in the oil field. Again and again, I had seen firsthand how dangerous oil and gas drilling can be. It seemed as though Al was always being hurt, but thankfully, he always got well. As I prayed for my wonderful husband, I was confident that he would be healed quickly and without any lasting ramifications

When I arrived at the hospital, Al was indeed seriously hurt once again! When the pipe fell on him, it left major cuts and gashes all over his body—including his neck and head. His body was covered with bruises. Most significantly, his right arm was broken and his right leg was fractured in his ankle and his knee. The fracture at his knee required major surgery and weeks of rehab. What on earth was taking place? Other men worked on the wells every day and were never hurt. Why does Al get seriously hurt repeatedly—again and again?

As a result of his injuries, he spent a full month in the hospital. The insurance policy I had purchased could not have come at a better time. The company paid $100 for each of the 30 days Al was hospitalized, and that helped us with our move to Tulsa. The decision to purchase that insurance was a good one!

This month in the hospital gave both of us time to think about the future. Al had worked hard to become one of the best in his work in the oil field. Hall-Jones had been good to us, but we knew that other companies were paying much more to their people who did the same work as Al. We knew it was time to investigate other opportunities. When we did, one of our major requirements was to remain in Oklahoma. A friend of ours in the oil business told us of an aggressive oil company in Tulsa named Exploration & Development Corporation. They were recruiting experienced individuals to join them in drilling and managing oil and gas fields. Al was tailor-made for that job!

The job offer at E & D came, and it meant a major financial increase for us. It also meant a move to Tulsa. We preferred to live in one of the suburbs of Tulsa, and settled on the bedroom community of Bixby, which was perfect for us.

CHAPTER TWELVE

THE SUPERNATURAL TIME IN BIXBY, OKLAHOMA

Our time in Bixby, Oklahoma was very active for us. We purchased a wonderful new home close to a great grade school for Steve and Brynda, who were in the fourth and third grades respectively. Sandi was almost three and demanded much of my time. Staying in our pattern, we quickly found the First Assembly of God Church and attended our first Sunday in Bixby. The pastors we had and the churches we attended over the last several years had strengthened our confidence in the Lord Jesus and led us to become more and more radical in our faith, but we were not expecting what was about to take place.

We loved our new home and our neighbors were wonderful. As was our tradition, if they weren't actively involved in a church, we invited them to attend with us. Some of our closest friends in the neighborhood were Joe and Donna Reeder. Joe was a Tulsa high school basketball coach and a delightful man to be around.

Joe and his entire family attended church with us during a revival, and they were radically born again. They were serious! They wanted all Christianity had for them, and more! They attended every possible Bible study and were at church for every service before the doors were even open. As a result of their excitement in the Lord Jesus, they became very caught up in "end time" studies and were convinced that each new event that happened was proof that the Lord Jesus was returning to the earth at any moment.

Crazy Neighbor

One night about midnight, our phone ran, waking us up from a deep sleep. I answered the phone, and on the other end of the line, our neighbor shouted, "Get up! Jesus is coming! Get up and watch the eastern sky!"

He was so convincing that I shook Al for him to wake up. As he was slowly coming out of his sleep, he said to me, "What's up? Who is calling?"

I said, "It's Joe Reeder, and he said Jesus is definitely coming this very minute! In fact, he said Jesus may have already come! We may have missed the rapture, and may have been left behind!" I was so excited I couldn't even think rationally!

I immediately handed Al the phone so I could go check on the children to see if they were in bed or gone. My heart was pounding out of my chest as I jumped out of bed and started running down the hallway. Earlier that day I had washed Steve's white tennis shoes and hung them to dry on the bathroom ceiling air vent. As I rushed past the darkened rooms, I glanced in the dark bathroom and saw the white shoes in the moonlight. I screamed, "Oh my God, there goes Steve!" I rushed back to our bedroom and told Al, "Steve's gone!"

Well, Al panicked and told Joe Reeder that indeed our baby boy was gone! In just a few moments, the Reeders' and their two children were ringing our door bell. When I opened the door, all four of them were standing there soaking wet having just walked two blocks from their house to ours in the pouring rain. They could not find their car keys and were not about to take time to look for them, so they walked.

By then, Al joined us in the living room and we were wondering what to do next. Joe asked me about Brynda, who was a small baby at that time, and I said, "I'm sure she's gone just like Steve."

Just to be sure, I ran back to her room and she was sleeping soundly in her baby bed. I ran back to the living room, and said, "Brynda is still here!" Then we were really puzzled. How can one baby be gone and one left?

So, we decided to call the pastor and see if he were still around. Finally, Al joined us in the conversation and said, "Wait! Don't call anyone. This doesn't make sense. If Jesus came, we should all be gone!" He looked at me and asked, "Are you sure Steve is gone?"

Then he turned and walked down the hall to Steve's room. In just a moment, he came back laughing and said, "You are all nuts! The kid is here! You are overreacting to the end time sermon we heard tonight. Let's all just relax," and then said with a big smile, "and I'll make some coffee." We all laughed about that night every time we got together.

Mud on the Boots

Things were not so confusing in Al's work. He was climbing the ladder of success in the oil and gas industry in his new position with E & D. The company was drilling several new wells across southern Kansas, and Al was supervising each of them. One of the rigs was drilling a great prospect right outside of the small town of Coldwater, Kansas. As his success in the oil field grew, he also grew spiritually. His love for and faith in the Lord Jesus was remarkable. Al developed a strong sense of the presence and leading of the Holy Spirit to such an extent that he was constantly praying for his workers and the strangers he met, and they were all healed and blessed. But even though he was experiencing powerful miracles, nothing could have prepared us for the major supernatural experience that Al would have in Coldwater.

One Wednesday night after spending the entire day at the drilling rig, Al left for his room at the Comanche Motel, and as was his practice, he showered and put on fresh clothes and his church boots and walked across the street to the Assembly of

God church to attend the Wednesday night service. Al enjoyed the service and even stood and gave a testimony of his love for the Lord Jesus and the great miracles he had been seeing. When the meeting finished, he met the young pastor and many of the people and thanked them for the wonderful service. He then returned to his room and laid across the bed, still fully clothed, to watch his favorite television show, *Gunsmoke.*

The next thing he knew, he was in a strange place which seemed to be a very wet and very dark jungle. He was literally encapsulated by thick impenetrable foliage, and as a result, could barely see his hand in front of his face. Every now and then, he would catch a glimpse of a small light flickering in the distance. Not knowing exactly what to do, he decided to fight his way through the leaves and vines and slowly make his way to the light. As he got closer, Al could see through the dense foliage several people moving around directly in front of him. Suddenly, he emerged from the jungle into a clearing filled with people. He had obviously stumbled into a small primitive village consisting of the "blackest" individuals he had ever seen.

Of course, Al had no idea where he was, but as he looked around the clearing, he saw an old man standing on the porch of a quaint looking, small house or hut, and when he did a young boy, maybe 13 or 14 years old, stood up next to him. When the old man stood, everyone turned and looked toward the old man as though they were awaiting instructions.

It was obvious that the old man was in charge of whatever was taking place with the people. So Al slowly walked through the crowd and up to the old man. The old man and the young boy looked at Al in utter disbelief! Not knowing what to do or say, Al began talking. He greeted them, told them who he was, and immediately gave them the same testimony about the miraculous power of Jesus to save and heal which he had just given in church that very night! Al told them he loved the Lord Jesus, had served the Lord for many years and had seen many great miracles. Al was not sure if they could understand him as he talked, but he continued sharing about Jesus.

As Al was speaking, the old man on the porch lifted his hand up and interrupted him. Then he proudly shouted at Al in English, "Our god is more powerful than your God! We can make people lame by sticking pins in a doll; we can make chickens talk, and we can even cause death!"

By this time, the crowd had gathered around the porch and completely encircled Al. The people grew more agitated by the minute. It was obvious they were not pleased by Al's presence and were not excited about his God. Al shouted back loudly for all to hear, "The Lord Jesus can heal your sick bodies, bring good things to you and give you life forever!"

The people began to shout back and forth with Al and each other for a few minutes until the old man screamed in anger and threw his staff at Al. The staff became a horrible giant snake hissing and striking at Al. The people ran back at the sight of the snake, but Al stood his ground, pointed at the snake and said, "In Jesus' Name, be still!"

Immediately, the snake shriveled and turned back into the wooden staff. The crowd gasped, started shouting curses at Al and began picking up stones and sticks to throw at him. When he saw what was happening, Al knew they were about to kill him, so he turned and ran back into the foliage the way he came.

As Al was running, he could hear people chasing him, and could tell they were closing in on him. Without knowing where he was going, he fought his way through the dense, dark foliage even harder. Soon, the sound of the crowd began to fade, and he could hear what sounded like only one person chasing him. When he slowed down and looked back, he saw it was the young boy he had seen on the porch with the old man. Al stopped to see why the boy was chasing him. Out of breath, the boy caught up with Al and acting like a typical teenager, asked, "Where is your car? Where is your car? I want to see your car! I want to see your car!"

"I don't have a car," Al responded with a shrug.

Confused, the young boy asked, "How did you get here?"

"I don't know... I have no idea!" Al said.

The boy immediately changed the subject, and said to Al, "Tell me more about your Jesus! You said He could do all this *good* stuff? In my village, we just know how to do bad stuff!"

Surrounded by the darkness of the foliage, Al told the young boy about some of the miracles God had done in his own life, and he shared with him how the Lord Jesus had died on the cross to save people from their sins. He told the young man that Jesus would forgive him and give him salvation so he could live forever in heaven.

About that time, Al heard the angry crowd again, and this time they were close. As he did, he turned around and saw an opening in the dense foliage and stepped into the opening. When he did, he was immediately in his motel room, lying across his bed.

It was daylight. Al was fully clothed and still had his church boots on. When he first sat up on the edge of the bed, he thought he had just awakened from a remarkable dream. However, when he looked down, he noticed some mud on his church boots. When Al worked in the fields, he always carried at least two pairs of boots, work boots and dress (cowboy) boots. These were his dress boots he had worn to church the night before. The mud was a puzzle. He had been to church in clean boots. There was no rain and he had certainly not stepped into some muddy puddle, yet now his church boots were extremely muddy.

He rose from the bed and got ready for work. When he was leaving the motel room, he glanced down and again saw his muddy church boots. For just a moment, he started to take time and clean the boots before he left, but then he changed his mind and took the church boots with him as he drove to the drilling rig.

On the drilling location was a mobile soils lab in which the geologists test the downhole formations through soil samples. Al entered the lab and set his mud covered dress boots against the wall of the lab and told the technician, "When you get a chance, check the mud on those boots, and see what you can find out about it."

Al told the tech nothing about the night before and went on up to the rig floor. Later that afternoon, one of the lab technicians came up and asked, "Al, where did you get that mud on your boots?"

"That's what you are supposed to tell me," Al responded.

"Umm, Mr. Wheeler? That type of soil on your boots is only found in East Africa."

"East Africa? I've never been to East Africa," Al insisted.

"Well, those boots have!" the tech demanded.

When Al returned to our home in Bixby, he told me his strange story. I didn't know exactly what to do. I believed what he said, but I was afraid of what he said. What would people say? How would they respond? What would they think of him if he shared it? I told him, "Don't tell anyone."

Al could not let it go. He told a close friend and neighbor, Joe Reeder, who was a coach in the Tulsa schools, and some of the men in the church, as well as our pastor. None of them took it seriously, and some told Al that he had just a weird dream and to forget about it, as he was sounding a little scary. So taking their advice Al dropped it, except every once in a while, when he wondered about the mud on his church boots!

THE TARGET

CHAPTER 13

HOME IN KINGFISHER

We were moving again. Work in the oil fields of Oklahoma was exploding with new discoveries and opportunities. The work at E & D Petroleum was expanding rapidly and so was Al's value and responsibility in the company. As always happens to families in the oil and gas business, when new oil and gas fields are found and drilled, the families who work the drilling rigs and make the wells productive must move to the new locations. The same was true for the engineers. By now, we were very familiar with the routine. This time the move was to the oil fields of western Oklahoma.

Our home in Bixby sold quickly so we were under pressure to find a place for our family. Steve was entering seventh grade, Brynda sixth grade and Sandi was just beginning kindergarten. This time we had money, so we decided to find the house that was centrally located to Al's work in which our children could spend the rest of their school days without another move. When we visited the various towns that would serve our purpose, we settled on Kingfisher, Oklahoma. Since it was located right in the middle of the oil and gas fields, many oil families called it home. Al could be anywhere in his work in less than a couple of hours. With its great schools, hospital, shopping and churches, Kingfisher welcomed new families.

We found a local realtor and began our search. It seemed as though every time he showed us a house, we went right by this large, historic, old, brown brick house with a red tile roof that was sitting abandoned right on Main Street. On one of our trips by the large house, Al asked, "What about that house?"

"Mr. Wheeler, you don't want to mess with that house," our realtor assured us. "It's large and drafty. The electric bills would be huge. The upkeep would be costly, and besides, it's controlled by a trust and would be a mess to deal with."

So, we dropped the thought of the historic house, at least for the moment.

The realtor kept pushing us toward a wonderful home complete with an indoor swimming pool, but Al could not stop thinking about the large historic home. A few days later we drove down Main Street to see another house, and of course, we went right by the historic house.

"Stop just a minute," Al insisted. "I want to look at that old house."

The realtor responded, "I don't have a key."

Al came back immediately, "Can't we just look in the windows?"

The realtor yielded, "Well, of course."

The house had obviously been abandoned for years. Weeds were everywhere. I was surprised the town had not made the owners take better care of the house even if it were empty. We approached the house from the street on the south side. A large bay window which dominated the entire wall was hidden by overgrown weeds and unkempt tree branches. The front of the house faced Main on the east and looked out over two large oak trees. The front porch ran the entire width of the house and was framed with four large columns that supported a balcony covering the porch. We made our way through the overgrown weeds and up on the front porch. The front door was in the middle of three beautiful, large glass doors that filled the north and south sides of the porch.

We both rubbed the dust off the window on the south side of the porch and peeked in. It was wonderful! We looked in at the remarkable living room with wood floors, gorgeous wood molding, and a magnificent fireplace with a 10-inch thick wooden mantle that stretched across the entire north wall of the living room. Even the canvas walls had hand-painted motifs on them!

"Can you get a key?" Al asked.

"Yes," the realtor said shaking his head affirmatively.

"We want to go to lunch," Al replied. "You drop us off at some place to eat, get a key and find out if this place is for sale, please."

"That sounds good, I'll do it," the realtor promised.

As we were eating a quick sandwich, the realtor returned. "I've got the key, and I'll know this afternoon if it is for sale," the realtor said as he walked to our table.

"Great," Al responded. "Let's go see it!"

The realtor walked us in the front door, and excused himself, and said, "Let me leave you alone for a few minutes. I need to go to my office and see if I've heard back from the owner about selling the house."

When he shut the door, we were alone in the historic home, and it felt good. We looked into every room and could picture our family enjoying this wonderful old house. The bedrooms were all upstairs. Steve can have this room. Brynda will be here. This can be Sandi's room. It was for us.

We went back downstairs and Al headed for the fireplace mantle. He laid his hands on the mantle, and prayed, "Lord, I claim this house in the name of the Lord Jesus Christ, and I thank you for giving it to us."

I responded, "Are you sure?"

"Yes," he said, "this is our house."

And he was right. In just a few moments, the realtor returned. "I've got good news. The owners are willing to sell."

Al stopped at that moment, and wrote him a check for half of the price of the house as down payment. "Wait," the realtor insisted, "you need a contract."

"You take care of that, and that's the earnest money," Al said with a big smile on his face!

Sure enough, in a few short days, the house was ours, and we began our life as a happy Kingfisher family living on Main Street.

Kingfisher Became Our New Home

As with each new place we lived, we visited several area churches and eventually chose the Church of the Nazarene which became our church for many years. The children were attending school, and I was busy putting together our new home and making new friends. The friends we made in Kingfisher became friends for life. I had no idea then, but those friends would be with me in some of my happiest moments, and ultimately see me through my most devastating and saddest days.

We thrived in Kingfisher, Oklahoma. Our children took to the new town as though they had lived there their entire lives. The old historic house was a delight to work on and decorate. And Al immediately began his new work and quickly rose to new levels of authority and opportunity with E & D Petroleum.

After about a year and a half with E & D, Al saw that he would be paid a great deal more if he worked as a consultant to several oil companies rather than an employee of a single company. One of the companies he worked with as a consultant was the Walker Company in Oklahoma City. He really liked Walker, and they liked him so much that they soon made him a terrific offer to join them as their in-house field supervisor. The position was made for Al. He directed the drilling and completion work on dozens of highly successful wells, and as a result, was given a portion of each well and a great salary. It meant absolute financial security for us and the opportunity for Al to continue to develop his knowledge and ability in the oil field. We were set for life! Thank you Jesus!

My problem with his time at the Walker Company was the sheer volume of his work. Al loved being in the oil field, and even though he had a beautiful office at the company headquarters in downtown Oklahoma City, Al was almost constantly in the field overseeing the wells. I kept complaining to the owners of the company, but the workload continued to grow.

Picture of the Headstone

On one of his times in the oil field, Al stopped at the cemetery in Ft. Cobb to visit the grave site of his mother and father. While there, he took a picture of their headstone which was a large, black marble stone with the name Wheeler written across the face of the stone. The picture of the headstone was on my desk as I filled out Al's monthly expense report which I sent to the company office for reimbursement. As I placed the report in the envelope, I accidentally included the picture of the headstone. When the envelope was opened in the headquarters, the financial secretary took the picture to the owner, Jim Walker. When

Jim saw the picture, he sent me a note that simply said, "I got the picture, and I really get it!"

I knew Al was overworking and needed to slow down. The children and I told him that many times, and he would always assure us that he would retire in time. We had purchased a big, beautiful farm that Al loved so much. He had every plan to retire and become a gentleman farmer. That was his dream!

Al always wanted a farm and a John Deere tractor. So one Christmas, which was his last Christmas, the kids and I planned a big surprise for their daddy. We opened gifts on Christmas Eve and had bought Al a toy John Deere tractor that ran by remote control. He loved the gift and immediately started scarring up the furniture legs. We asked him how he liked his gift and he said, "I love it, but I was hoping for something a little bit bigger!" At that moment, Brynda brought in a child's riding John Deere. Al got a real kick out of that, sat on the seat and pushed it across the floor.

Then the kids and I said, "Let's go to the farm and turn off all the Christmas lights out there."

Al agreed, "Great, let's go!"

So we drove five miles to the farm and turned out the Christmas lights around the house. Al said, "It looks like there are lights on in the barn. Let's turn those off."

We all walked down to the barn and Al pressed the button to open the huge electric doors. Inside was his real Christmas surprise! A brand new, bright green and yellow 4440 John Deere tractor! He was overwhelmed! He wanted to drive it right then, but it was freezing and we nixed that until morning.

The first day Al was off work, he left the house at 6:00 a.m. to go to the farm. He started working the land, fertilizing it and sowing wheat. He had no idea what he was doing, but he said he had watched farmers plant wheat and did what they did. He would plant for about 30 minutes, then get off the tractor and go to the seed box on the back, open the lid and check the seed. I asked him what he was doing, and he said, "I have no idea, but I have seen farmers stop their tractors, get out and check the seed box. So, that's what I'm doing!" Finally, a farmer told him he didn't need to check his seed box until he had planted long enough to be about out of seed which could take a few hours. I believe he simply enjoyed stopping and getting off the tractor so he could look at the tractor. After all, it was the biggest toy he ever owned!

Flowing with the Holy Spirit

As Al continued to develop in the oil and gas business, he moved deeper and deeper into the supernatural ministry of the Holy Spirit. His faith and confidence in the Lord Jesus was amazing. We spoke of the African translation many times, and he was convinced it was a true experience. The muddy boots continued to be the proof he relied upon. While we were in Kingfisher, the translations continued. He shared some with me, but not each of them. I think he was concerned he would frighten me. Other people told us of seeing him in some ministry situation in far-off places, but he never told us. He told me one night that he was often translated and confessed, "Sometimes I'm afraid I will get out there and not be able to get back!"

One translation occurred in 1981. I received a call from my brother Ronnie that my mother was seriously ill and was in the hospital awaiting emergency surgery. Gangrene had set up in her body, and we were told it was a life-threatening situation. I immediately called Al, who was in the far northern part of Oklahoma drilling an oil well over five hours from the hospital. He was at a place in the drilling where he could not leave the well because if anything went wrong, it could blow out the well and cause a huge fire or worse. He assured me he would be there as soon as possible.

Mother asked me right before her surgery, "Please tell Albert to come and have him pray for me." Mother always had great faith in Al's prayers and called him when she needed someone to pray. I knew she would be disappointed that Al could not be there, so I assured her Al would come.

I waited tearfully and prayerfully for the surgery to be completed along with my dad, brothers and their wives. At long last, the doctor came and told us the surgery was successful and mother was in recovery. When I saw her in recovery, the first thing I said was, "Mom, I'm so sorry, but Al could not come during your surgery, but he will be here as soon as he can."

She looked at me kind of puzzled and said, "Why, Albert was here. They let him come in the operating room. He prayed for me and told me, 'Mom, don't worry, you are going to get well and live another fifteen years.'"

I said, "No Mom, he wasn't here."

She disagreed, "Yes, he was! And he told me to look around the room at all the angels. I saw a dozen angels standing at my bed, all dressed in white."

Another amazing thing happened while Mother was hospitalized. When Al told friends and business partners what was happening with his mother-in-law and how he wished he could be there, they all began sending flowers to the hospital. When Mom was taken to her room, all around the head of her bed were 12 bouquets of flowers and each of the bouquets was white! It looked like twelve angels in white standing sentinel at her bed.

The flowers came from all over. What is the chance of 12 white bouquets? God has a plan and a purpose. He does all things well!

Over the succeeding years, Mom experienced many deaths around her. Al died in 1983, her son Ronnie in 1985, and her husband in 1989. But she lived until May 14, 1996. Just as Al told her that night in the operating room, she lived a full and healthy 15 more years.

CHAPTER 14

THE VALIDATING MEETING

O ur growing commitment to the Lord Jesus and our financial success opened a variety of opportunities for us to support various ministries in which we believed. One of those ministries was with Melodyland School of Theology in Anaheim, California. Al loved the school because it was training men and women for the ministry and sending them around the world to preach and minister in the name of the Lord Jesus. Al was asked to serve on the board of trustees.

The relationship with the school began a friendship with Pastor Ralph Wilkerson, who was the pastor of Melodyland Christian Center. Each summer, Melodyland conducted a Spirit Conference which brought leaders across the charismatic world to the church for a week. The conference was wonderful! It allowed us to meet and become friends with many of these outstanding men and women who were leading the church and changing the world, but we were not prepared to meet one single, young man who changed our lives forever.

Between the two morning sessions, we were standing in the hallway that circled the major auditorium at Melodyland, trying to decide which session to attend next. As we were talking and deciding, a young African couple in beautiful African dress was walking toward us in the hallway. I noticed that Al kept staring at the young man and the young man was staring back at Al.

"Do you know him?" I said, seeking to get Al's attention.

"I don't know," Al replied, "but I think I do."

By this time, the African couple had stopped. Al pointed toward the young man, and asked, "Do I know you?"

"I think I know you," the young man replied.

"Have I met you before?" Al asked again.

"Yes!" the young man replied. "You are the man who came to my village in Uganda."

Al shook his head, and insisted, "I've never been to Uganda."

"Yes, yes you have!" the young man demanded. "You are the man who came to my village through the jungle. I'm the young boy who was standing with my uncle who was the witch doctor standing on the porch of our hut. You're the man who rebuked the snake!"

"Yes," Al said, erupting with excitement! "It's you! It's you!"

After a moment of shouting and rejoicing, Al asked, "What is your name?"

"Joel Walehwa," the young man answered.

"I'm Al, Al Wheeler."

"Nice to know your name, Mr. Wheeler," Joel responded.

Al turned and introduced me, and the young man introduced his wife. We all greeted one another and hugged and hugged! It seemed we all knew that we would forever be joined together. The Lord Jesus had orchestrated our meeting, and none of us knew in that moment where our relationship was going to take us, but we knew it was a supernatural moment.

I stood there not believing what was happening. After all these years and despite all the rebukes and unbelief he endured, Al had always maintained that he was indeed translated to Africa. The mud on his boots was his inescapable proof. But now, we were meeting face to face with the eyewitness who had been with him that night in Uganda. I started to weep with joy!

"We must get together," Al insisted.

"Yes, yes, where can I meet you?" the young man asked.

"Across the street at the hotel," Al said. "Let me take you and your wife to lunch."

"Yes, we will be there."

We could not wait for the morning session to be over and our lunch to begin. Al was excited, but cautious. He had his strategy for the meeting.

"I'm not going to tell him what I experienced; I want him to tell me what I experienced. Let's see if our stories match," Al demanded.

When we arrived at the hotel for lunch after the morning session, Joel and his lovely wife were waiting. Al secured a large round booth for us. Our two daughters, Brynda and Sandi joined us, and the conversation began. Al spoke first, "Joel, how did you get here at Melodyland?"

Ironically, he was attending Melodyland School of Theology on scholarship and Al and I were providing scholarships for the school. So in a way, we were sponsoring the young African that Al had met in Uganda. Only God could have put all this together! Joel was born and reared in Uganda, had a degree, and had been a teacher to Idi Amin's children. Now his passion was spreading the gospel of Jesus Christ.

"That's wonderful," Al said, "but Joel, I want you to tell me what happened that night. Tell me everything you remember. I don't want to coach you in any way. You start."

Joel was not hesitant. Through his broken English, Joel told the story of that remarkable night. At age 13, Joel was studying to be a witch doctor under the tutorage of his uncle who was the head witch doctor in his village. On the evening that Al came to his village, people were preparing for the annual festival in which a child would be sacrificed to the giant snake that lived in and around a large tree at the heart of the village. As the celebration was beginning and the child was about to be killed, Al walked into the village from out of the jungle.

Joel told of Al simply appearing in his village and telling his uncle about Jesus. His uncle became hostile because he was the witch doctor and did not want anyone spoiling his territory. He threw his walking stick down on the ground and the stick became the giant snake. Remember, Joel insisted, the snake hissed and struck at you, and you stepped back and demanded, "In Jesus' name, be still!"

"When you did," Joel said with his eyes squarely on Al, "the snake became the stick again."

Joel assured us that the giant snake was never seen again in the village and no other child was ever sacrificed. "We knew that the power of Jesus had come to our village, and we were never the same."

Joel shared that his mother had constantly encouraged him to read the Bible a missionary had given her. He read some of it, but he was more interested in becoming a witch doctor. Already, even as a young teenager, he could make chickens speak and could put together active voodoo dolls.

Every detail of his story matched perfectly with what Al had said took place.

We were all thrilled. Joel had validated the supernatural translation event. We all visited for hours, stunned by the revelation.

Joel then shared with us that he was banned from returning to Uganda because of an incident involving the disappearance of one of his little students. Joel had been hired to teach Idi Amin's children. One day, Amin's little daughter suddenly quit coming to class. When Joel asked her brother about her absence, the brother said, "My dad sacrificed her to the crocodiles."

When Joel launched an investigation, he received a visit from Amin's people and was told to leave the country and never come back at risk of his life and the lives of others.

Al sat there very quietly, and then said something that shocked all of us to our core. "Joel," he said with great certainty, "I hear the Holy Spirit saying, 'Within seven days, you will be in Uganda standing in front of Idi Amin.'"

Then he continued, "When this happens, you and I both will know that the experience we had in Uganda that night was a reality and not a dream or vision. I don't know why this translation happened, but I think it will be a tool that will be mightily used by the Lord Jesus through the church at some time. It happened to Jesus and to Philip with the Eunuch. Jesus said that we would do what He did and even greater things because He returned to the Father and sent the Holy Spirit (John 14:12). I believe this supernatural manifestation will be seen more and more in the church!"

Joel almost passed out when Al made this statement about his being in front of Idi Amin.

"Mr. Wheeler, I can't!" he insisted. "I have a wife and small children to care for. My family is still in Uganda; they will be killed. My uncle is an officer in Amin's headquarters. It will cause him to be killed if I return. He is the one who helped me get away from Amin and out of the country. I can't go back!"

Al softly replied, "All I am saying is what I heard in my spirit, and I know it was from the Holy Spirit."

Al reached for his billfold and gave Joel a gift, and said, "I want you to have this." Later, Joel would say it was the first time he had ever received a $100 bill. He was very thankful! Al invited him to come to Oklahoma and visit as soon as he returned from Uganda. We parted with Joel's last words, "Mr. Wheeler, I'm sorry, but I won't be going to Uganda."

Al said, "Bless you! I'll be praying for you."

I wondered if we would ever see Joel again, but a few days later, he called us and said in his normally overexcited voice, "You won't believe this, but I'm going back to Uganda tomorrow!"

He told us that the day after meeting with us, he was asked to go into Pastor Wilkerson's office. When he entered the office the pastor asked him, "Joel, aren't you from Uganda, and don't you have a connection with Idi Amin?"

Joel replied, "Yes, but—"

Pastor Wilkerson broke in, "The Lord spoke to me and said I must go pray for this terrorist leader. I understand you have a relative working in his headquarters. Do you think you could get us in?"

Joel said, "Well, maybe I could make a call to my uncle. When do you want to go?"

The pastor said, "Tomorrow!"

Joel almost fell over. He was thinking the trip might be planned for months ahead. Joel called his uncle, and made an appointment for Pastor Wilkerson to see Amin in two days. The pastor insisted that Joel go with them to assist with speech translation. So the next day, Pastor Wilkerson, Joel and a few other leaders left for Uganda. When Joel stood before Amin, it was on the seventh day after his visit with Al, just as Al had prophesied. This was just one of many of Al's prophesies we saw fulfilled.

Nick and the White House

Al and I always tithed from the very beginning of our marriage, but with the growing success Al experienced in oil and gas, we were able to financially share in the lives and ministries of several individuals. One of our favorite ministries was that of Nick and Pauline Cadena, Fellowship Prison Ministries in Pasadena, California. Nick was convicted of murder and heroin distribution and spent 20 years in prison. While he was in prison, he received Jesus as Lord and Savior through the ministry of Kathryn Kuhlman. Coming out of prison, Nick and Pauline launched a wonderful prison ministry and opened two large homes in Pasadena to assist individuals coming out of prison.

Nick and Pauline came to our home in Kingfisher several times, and each time they brought some of the young former convicts with them. These men worked the entire time they were with us. The sidewalks were constantly swept, our cars were washed and polished, as well as many other tasks Nick could find for them to do.

We did find out the hard way to not allow them to operate any of our oilfield equipment. I think Al thought their prison time qualified them for the hard work of the oilfield. Not so!

On one of their visits, we received an invitation from President and Mrs. Ronald Reagan to visit Washington, D.C. and the White House for a fun-filled weekend as members of the elite Republican Eagles. Al mentioned to me that he would like to take Nick Cadena to the White House with us and introduce him to the president. I exclaimed, "You are kidding! This man is a convicted felon charged with murder and spent 15 years in prison. There is no way he could be cleared for the White House."

I put that thought right out of my mind, but a few days later, Al said, "Well, Nick Cadena is going to the White House with us."

"How did that happen?" I replied. "Stop! I don't even want to know."

Sure enough, one bright fall day, Al, Nick, our son, Steve, and our daughter Sandi and I flew to Washington, D.C. Brynda was in graduate school and could not go. We visited our senator, Don Nickels. Then we dressed in our finest and proceeded to the White House. I must say that our friend Nick was undoubtedly one of the most handsome men there in his fine black tux, but he had a look on his face all weekend like, "What am I doing here?"

We had a wonderful dinner and then went into the ballroom and danced. Sandi met Nancy Reagan and said to her,

"You are so beautiful."

And Nancy replied, "So are you, young lady."

I must say that I was terrified to dance with President Reagan! I was afraid I would step on his shoes or trip him somehow. Al was his usual confident self, and had no problem dancing with Nancy. Nick just stayed close to the children. I don't really think he could believe where he was and what was happening.

Many years later after losing Al, I visited with the Cadenas in their California home. The first thing I noticed in their main room was a large photo of Nick and Al standing with President Reagan. Nick got a lot of mileage out of that story, and Al never tired of telling how he took a convicted felon to a presidential party in the White House. Al always had a knack for accomplishing the impossible!

CHAPTER 15

THE EAGLE HAS FLOWN

The long, sleepless hours of Friday night mercifully ended. It was Saturday. In a few short hours, my family would experience the funeral of the one who was my husband, father of my children, and also my best friend. I was not sure how we would make it, but we would.

Around 7:00 a.m., I smelled coffee and heard the first sounds of friends in my kitchen preparing to serve all those who would visit our home on that tragically sad day. I managed to force myself out of bed, found my house robe and slowly walked downstairs. As soon as I entered my kitchen, at least a dozen of my friends were present who had arrived early that morning to make sure everything would be in place, and they would be there all day to care for me and my family. We all gathered around the breakfast bar in the kitchen, where we had gathered scores of times through the years.

Each one wanted to know how I was doing, did I need anything, was there anything they could do for me. Again and again, they expressed their love and prayers for me and my children, and how deeply sorry they were for the unthinkable loss of Al. The love and care for me throughout that day was wonderful, but once again, I could not eat. Coffee was still the only thing that I could manage to get down.

Brynda joined me and the others in the kitchen and reminded me that my hair dresser, Carol, would arrive at 9:00 a.m. to shampoo and style my hair. I returned upstairs and finished showering and washing my hair just as she arrived. While Carol was busy working on my hair, Brynda placed a white pill in front of me and instructed me to take it.

"What is it?" I asked.

"Just take it," was Brynda's response. I obeyed. I'm sure it was some sort of tranquilizer, but I didn't need it. I was already numb to everything going on around me.

During the days immediately following Al's death, my role with Brynda switched. She watched over me as I had always done over her, and she seemed to always know what to do. Her strength and wisdom were remarkable and very comforting to me.

After Carol finished my hair, I entered our bedroom to dress for the funeral. I knew exactly what I wanted to wear. Two weeks earlier, I had purchased a fabulous two-piece suit which consisted of a black skirt and the most beautiful top. The fabric was made of hundreds of small, brightly colored triangles. I thought it was absolutely gorgeous! When I brought it home, Al loved it.

"I can't wait to see you wear that," he said with obvious approval.

"Do you want me to try it on right now for you?" I asked.

"No, wait and surprise me with it on the right occasion," he replied. "You'll know when it's time to wear it."

And I did. I bought it to please him; now I would wear it to honor him. At the funeral, many remarked how beautiful the suit was. Every time they did, I simply smiled and said, "I'm wearing it for Al."

Heading to the Funeral

The funeral was scheduled for 2:00 p.m. at our church, the First Nazarene Church in Kingfisher. Except for our own home, the church was the most important place in our lives. We loved our church, and the church loved us. They could not have been more caring to us throughout the ordeal of Al's death.

The long black limousine pulled up to our house at exactly 11:30 a.m. to take us to the church where a wonderful meal had been prepared for the entire family. The limousine was large enough to accommodate my mother and father, Steve, Brynda, Sandi and her husband, Brett, and me.

We departed our home together, and as we did, we all paused, and for some reason looked back at the wonderful house that had been our beloved home for many years. No one was speaking but, in just a moment, Brynda broke the silence, "Look at the rose!"

A single red rose had bloomed on a rose bush on the south side of our house. For most families, the rose would have had no meaning, but for us it was supernatural. Al loved roses, and in fact, his nickname as a kid was "Rosie" because of his rosy cheeks.

When we moved into the house and decided how our yards would be landscaped, Al insisted on making a rose garden on the south side to take advantage of the sun. It was his garden. For years he planted beautiful rose bushes, weeded the garden, made sure the soil was perfect, fertilized and pampered each bush. The bushes leafed out each year, but there were never any roses, not one single rose! I wanted Al to tear the bushes out and replace them with lilacs or something that would actually bloom. I was tired of bloomless rosebushes, all green and never a bloom. Al would only say, "You watch, someday they will bloom!"

Now, as we left the house for the funeral, there was a single red rose. For us, it was a sign that Al was in a good place, a place he wanted to be. It was also a sign that we would be OK. Each of us stood transfixed for a moment. That bush, nor the others, ever bloomed again.

Reality Struck

Ultimately, it was happening. Something I never dreamed would take place. I had entered the limousine that would take me to bury the body of my husband. The ride to the church from our house was only a few minutes. Not a word was said. When we drove up to the door of the church, Brett stepped out first and immediately turned back and offered his hand to Sandi, and then Steve left the limousine and leaned back inside to help Brynda and me. Finally, my parents were assisted from the limousine by both Steve and Brett.

The seven of us stood for a moment, almost as if we did not know our way into the church. Within seconds, Keith Maule, the pastor of First Nazarene, was there, greeting us and ushering us into the room where the meal was prepared and our extended family was awaiting our arrival. Despite the short notice of only two days, our entire extended family was present: Al's brothers and sisters and their families, nephews, nieces, and grandchildren and my four brothers and their wives and children. The family tables filled the fellowship hall, and spilled out into the hallway and part of the auditorium. Three of our favorite pastors from the past and their families, who were there to participate in the service, were also present. The church did a remarkable job preparing and serving the huge family meal.

I placed a few small pieces of food on my plate, but I could not eat. Repeatedly I was encouraged to eat, but it was impossible. My mind and heart were filled with reoccurring thoughts. Our lives always revolved around Al. We moved where he needed. When he was gone, we waited for him. When he was home, we rejoiced and enjoyed our lives with him. He planned our lives, filled our lives and made our lives exciting and fulfilling. How could this happen? Now, what would we do? Could I lead us, keep us together, continue the life he had provided for us? Little wonder I could not eat!

As the family was finishing lunch, Gene Massey, a local pastor who was a longtime friend to Al and me, asked all of us to make our way into the auditorium. Pastor Massey and Ken Gaub from Seattle, another pastor who was a close friend to Al and me, wanted to spend time with the family prior to the funeral. They both genuinely prayed for us and attempted to encourage us to stay close to one another and to the Lord Jesus. Their words were good. Pastor Massey spoke glowingly of Al, both as his friend and an employer. Pastor Ken Gaub had known Al for many years. His words to the family were wonderful. The last time they were together Al gave Ken a gold horse-head ring. Al loved the ring and wore it every day for several years, but when they were together, Al took off the ring and gave it to Ken and said, "I think you will get more wear out of this ring than I will."

At first, Ken refused to accept the ring, but Al insisted. "Now," Ken told the family, "I wear it every day." Ken still wears the ring 33 years later.

It was a precious family time which gave all of us opportunity to weep and remember, before facing the ordeal of the funeral. Finally, it was time. The funeral director gave us instructions about entering the church gymnasium and where we would be seated. When we walked out of the auditorium where the family had been meeting and into the hallway, the church was so overflowing with people that the hallway was entirely filled. We had decided on using the church gymnasium for the service because it was larger, but it was not large enough. People were everywhere.

The music began and the usher opened the door to the gym. Flowers filled the room, hundreds of flowers from individuals, families and oil companies across the nation. As soon as we entered the room, I saw the casket. I had seen it before but not in this setting, literally surrounded by flowers and hundreds of people. When I saw it, it took my breath away and for a quick moment, I thought I might faint, but my two wonderful daughters both held me tightly.

Brynda and Sandi stood on each side of me with Steve and Brett assisting my mom and dad right behind us. We entered the gym and walked slowly down the center aisle to our assigned seats. They seated the family on bleachers as close to the front side as possible. When we reached our place, the seven of us took our seats while those present stood and waited for the seating of our extended family.

In one respect, I did not like where we were seated because we were so exposed and visible. But as the service continued, I began to look back at those gathered and it was wonderful to see the ones who came from across the nation. When I would catch the eye of some friend, they would say without uttering a word, "I am so sorry, and I am with you." I was deeply blessed by their presence.

Once the family was seated, Pastor Keith Maule came to lead the congregation in prayer. We loved Pastor Maule. Years earlier, our family had joined First Nazarene, and Pastor Keith had become very important to our lives, and we were to his. His prayer that day was a prayer of thankfulness for Al, and a prayer of blessing for us. I prayed along with him and cried out to the Lord for His protection and help.

Al's Homegoing Ceremony

The service was wonderful in every way. The youth pastor of First Nazarene was a gifted singer and had agreed to sing a song Al loved, called "Where No Man Stands Alone." It was difficult for him to find the music, but he did. I did not remember how sad the song was until I heard it that day, but it could not have been more appropriate.

Our wonderful friend and former pastor in Hill City, Kansas, Rev. Dan McGraw, who had prayed with Al to be baptized in the Holy Spirit, read the obituary and prayed. Then three sisters in our church sang Al's favorite song "What a Day That Will Be." Before they sang, they told the congregation that Al loved the song, but felt it needed another verse for it to be complete. So, Al wrote a last verse, and they sang it. Perfectly!

Then Pastor Keith came to speak. It was not an easy task for him. He knew Al well and was forced to fight back tears throughout his sermon. He began by saying that Al was the most unique man he had ever met, a man who never met a stranger, and then proceeded to tell stories from Al's life that proved his point. He spoke of Al's great faith and the many times the Lord Jesus had used him to heal individuals and save lives.

The pastor told the events of the previous New Year's Eve when Al and I were on our way to a party in Oklahoma City. As we were approaching the small town of Okarche, we came upon a wreck. A car had run into a tree, and a young woman had been thrown from her car through the windshield. We were the first to reach the accident. Al stopped and immediately ran to help. When he reached the girl, her face and head had been severely cut, and she was losing blood. She was within minutes of bleeding to death. Al quickly found the cuts on her face and in her hair and held them together with his hands to stop the bleeding, and began to pray. When the ambulance arrived, Al told the medics to take her to the hospital, and that he was not going to turn her loose until they arrived at the emergency room. He saved her life. When the Pastor told that story, a couple stood up in the funeral and testified, "We are the parents of that girl. Al saved her life!"

Pastor Keith continued. Al was not just about heroics; he was mainly about love. Al loved Jesus, and because he loved Jesus, he loved others. Al especially loved his family. The pastor spoke of the many times he had been with Al and heard him speak of his great love he had for me and our children, and all the confidence he had in each of them and their futures. Pastor Keith assured the congregation that day that Al's love was not limited to his own family. Then he told the story of the candy Al always had in his pocket.

"Each Sunday, Al would bring a sucker or a peppermint candy to church, and when my little 2-year-old son, Ryan, would see Al, he would run to him. Al would pick him up and say, 'Ryan, look what I've got for you.'"

Al would reach in his pocket and find that piece of candy and say, "This is just for you." And Ryan would squeal with delight.

Pastor Keith paused a minute, and fighting tears from his eyes, he said softly, "You know why I loved Al, because he so loved my little son." There was not a dry eye in the house!

The pastor gave one great closing illustration. He spoke of growing up in San Diego and loving to visit the world-famous zoo. He said he did not go to see the lions or the elephants or even the monkeys; rather, he loved to watch the eagles.

"I would watch these great birds which were meant to soar to the highest heights, walking around on the ground. But every now and then, one of them would take off and begin to fly in this enormous cage that had been built just for them. But they could only go so high. On their leg was placed a tether, and every time they would begin to soar, the tether would take hold and yank them back down to earth."

Pastor Keith drew the parallel with Al. God had shown him remarkable, supernatural truths and allowed him to have amazing, miraculous experiences; but every time he would begin to soar to the new astounding heights, the tether would take hold and Al would be yanked back down.

"Well," Pastor Keith proclaimed, "The only difference between today and two days ago is that the tether has been cut, and the eagle has flown! Now, and for eternity, there are no limits!"

CHAPTER 16

FINDING ANSWERS

We returned to our home from the cemetery late Saturday afternoon, and finally after 48 straight hours, the house was empty again. My friends would stay close and love me through the coming years, but none of them had what I needed most: answers!

As I sat on my sofa that sad night, the question I shouted at God on Thursday when I learned of Al's tragic death remained, "How could you do this to me?"

How could Al Wheeler, a man who loved the Lord Jesus, who served the Lord Jesus, who loved others, who gave so much to bless the church and pastors and others with needs, how could he be killed in the prime of his life? Fears regarding the future remained, but my real questions were not about money or security. My questions were about God.

Al and I loved the Lord Jesus with all our hearts. Because of that love and the purity of our faith and confidence in the presence and power of the Holy Spirit, we opened our lives to everything the Lord Jesus desired to do with us and through us. And it was awesome!

We experienced the true blessings of the Lord, and walked into areas of the supernatural that few have experienced. I believe with all my heart that Al was chosen by the Lord as a man through whom He desired to do greater and greater things. The Lord Jesus was certainly not through with Al when he died. It was not the will of God that he was killed.

But we did not have adequate teaching in those days. We did not know the truth.

I am not being negative about those who taught us and pastored us. We loved them and learned a great deal from them. I will always be grateful to them for everything they poured into each of us. But they were not able to teach us because they did not know themselves what we needed. No one in our lives knew what we were experiencing and the ramifications of where Al was walking in the supernatural. Therefore, we were walking and living blind!

Al and I always believed that if an individual or family loved the Lord Jesus and lived a faithful life of obedience and surrender to the will of the Lord, everything would be good. That was the life we lived. Everything in our life was blessed! We constantly claimed promises of blessing and lived fully expecting the protection of God in our lives.

One of the great promises I stood on is found in the commandment, "Honour thy father and thy mother: that thy days may be long upon the land which the Lord thy God giveth thee" (Ex. 20:12). If he were late getting home from his work on a drilling rig, I would sit in my window where I could watch for him and remind the Lord of how much he loved, cared for and honored both his parents and mine. I never knew anyone who loved their parents as much Al loved his. Therefore, he had to be safe and live a long life.

We knew there was a devil, but the possibility of any type of overt satanic attack against our life was never considered a threat. We never talked about it. When Al would be hurt, we only saw it as an accident. There was nothing satanic or demonic behind an injury; it was just the way the world worked. Our confidence was in the will of God and His sovereign choices over our lives. We never considered for a moment that we could be attacked in such a brutal way, but we were wrong!

When we first started to be active in ministry, we were so naïve. Although it was never a concern to us, we believed there was a protective covering over our lives. Nothing could harm us!

It has taken years, hours and hours of searching and questioning, of listening and challenging, but for me at least, I have settled on answers. And I believe I am right! I have come to believe that the deeper and deeper an individual goes in their commitment to the work of the Lord Jesus and His Church and the more and more that an individual opens his or her life to the supernatural work of the Holy Spirit, the greater threat they become to the work of the devil and his kingdom of darkness. When that takes place, that individual becomes a target for the one who desires to steal, kill and destroy (John 10:10).

This does not mean that Christians should be afraid of the work or power of the devil, but it does mean Christians should be aware of the work of darkness and know how to thwart that work. The New Testament is replete with warnings concerning the demonic kingdom and its strategy against the Christian, especially against those who are committed to the work of the ministry. Satan focuses most of his attacks against the work of the church. Where the ministry of the church is advancing, there the kingdom of darkness will be fighting!

The Apostle Paul experienced this demonic opposition throughout his ministry and ultimately in his death. He believed demonic forces were at work, provoking the crowds and authorities to crucify the Lord Jesus (1 Cor. 2:8). The apostle told the Thessalonians that he and his companions wanted to come to them "once and again; but Satan hindered us" (1 Thess. 2:18). He consistently prayed that leaders would be protected "from the evil one" (2 Thess. 3:2-3).

Now, I look back on Al's life, and I see that from the very beginning he was a target. He was seriously hurt many times, and yet we never understood what was happening. I realize that we were totally unaware of the spiritual seriousness of what the reoccurring injuries meant. I am embarrassed to admit that we used to tease Al when he would be hurt and proclaim that he was accident-prone. Now I understand, he was not accident-prone;

he was repeatedly under attack as the devil attempted to destroy him. He was a target, a very big target, and we were not fighting back! Since we were not aware and not fighting back, he was killed.

Since his death, Kenneth and Gloria Copeland have become friends to our family. On one occasion, Kenneth told me that if he would have known us when Al was alive, Al would not have died. When Kenneth said that, I really did not understand what he meant. But now, I believe what he said is true! I am certain he would have known Al was a target and would have known how to prepare us for the fight.

I further believe that it is essential for the Christian to understand life as a life of battles with genuine enemies who possess the ability to kill. As a result, Christian victory is never the result of passivity and never happens without conflict. Before Al was killed, I believed that real conflict was totally unnecessary for an individual who was following Jesus as Lord and Savior; but now, I realize that nothing could be further from the truth. Throughout the New Testament, the concept of Christians in battle is a reoccurring theme. Jesus warns His disciples to expect conflict. The Apostle Paul instructs the church to put on the whole armor of God and be prepared to stand against the onslaught of the enemy and in the Revelation, the church is pictured as following Jesus into battle.

The great distinction in the battles fought by Christians is the possibility of absolute victory. But if a Christian is unaware of the true enemy he or she faces and does not know when and how to fight, that individual will experience life as a series of tragic, unnecessary defeats and even death.

I never fully understood the importance of the teaching of the Apostle Paul when he demanded that we put on the full armor of God, and stand firm against the schemes of the devil, and having done everything to stand firm, stand (Eph. 6:11-14)! Since the death of my precious Al, I have devoured the Scripture and have come to believe that he was a target that Satan desired to kill many times. Tragically, we never knew the reality behind the attacks, and therefore we did not arm ourselves to stand against the "schemes of the devil."

Today is different! I never begin my day without praying and claiming the protective hedge of the Holy Spirit about me and my family. I purposely command Satan and every demonic force to leave me, my family and those I love, alone. I break every demonic assignment or strategy that has been made against me and my family. I claim the power of the blood of the Lord Jesus over my life and the provision and protection of the Lord for my day. I refuse to be caught off guard!

I accept the fact that the Christian life is a battle. But it is a battle the Christian can and will win, if he or she will fight. And I fight!

I will never sit in my window and passively wait again and let someone I love be attacked or destroyed without a fight. If Al were still alive and he were late arriving home, I would start praying and doing battle. I would leave nothing to chance, and I would leave no area uncovered in which Satan could have an entrance to harm or kill him. I would not stop until I saw his car turn the corner and into our driveway.

My greatest motivation in writing this book is to proclaim this truth. We have an enemy! The enemy is not in any way greater than the Lord Jesus, but the enemy does have power and must be confronted. Each Christian who is committed to the work of the Lord Jesus and the supernatural ministry of the Holy Spirit must know without question that he or she is a target. However, if a follower of Jesus understands the ways of the enemy and the strategy of Christian warfare and fights, victory is certain!

I am determined to live in that victory, and I want each Christian to do so. Blessings on you as you stand in victory!

PRAYER OF SALVATION

God loves you—no matter who you are, no matter what your past. God loves you so much that He gave His one and only begotten Son for you. The Bible tells us that "...whoever believes in Him shall not perish but have eternal life" (John 3:16 NIV). Jesus laid down His life and rose again so that we could spend eternity with Him in heaven and experience His absolute best on earth. If you would like to receive Jesus into your life, say the following prayer out loud and mean it from your heart.

Heavenly Father, I come to You admitting that I am a sinner. Right now, I choose to turn away from sin, and I ask You to cleanse me of all unrighteousness. I believe that Your Son, Jesus, died on the cross to take away my sins. I also believe that He rose again from the dead so that I might be forgiven of my sins and made righteous through faith in Him. I call upon the name of Jesus Christ to be the Savior and Lord of my life. Jesus, I choose to follow You and ask that You fill me with the power of the Holy Spirit. I declare that right now I am a child of God. I am free from sin and full of the righteousness of God. I am saved in Jesus' name. Amen.

If you prayed this prayer to receive Jesus Christ as your Savior for the first time, please contact us on the Web at **www.harrisonhouse.com** to receive a free book.

Or you may write to us at

Harrison House • P.O. Box 35035 • Tulsa, Oklahoma 74153

The Harrison House Vision

Proclaiming the truth and the power

Of the Gospel of Jesus Christ

With excellence;

Challenging Christians to

Live victoriously,

Grow spiritually,

Know God intimately.

Fast. Easy. Convenient.

For the latest Harrison House product information and author news, look no further than your computer. All the details on our powerful, life-changing products are just a click away. New releases, E-mail subscriptions, testimonies, monthly specials — find it all in one place. Visit harrisonhouse.com today!

harrisonhouse